Healing
LIVES
(II)

Another One Hundred True Stories
of Encouragement and Achievement
in the Midst of Sickness!

TOBE MOMAH M.D.

WESTBOW
PRESS®
A DIVISION OF THOMAS NELSON
& ZONDERVAN

WestBow Press books may be ordered through booksellers or by contacting:

WestBow Press
A Division of Thomas Nelson & Zondervan
1663 Liberty Drive
Bloomington, IN 47403
www.westbowpress.com
1 (866) 928-1240

Scriptures are taken from the King James Version of the Bible.

ISBN: 978-1-5127-7753-6 (sc)

Print information available on the last page.

WestBow Press rev. date: 3/24/2017

It is not about the healing: it is about the journey to the healing!

I dedicate this book to Rita Momah; she is a doyen of womanhood, a quintessential embodiment of femininity, a person per excellence and a shower of blessings to my life. Thank you for your love, patience and goodness and may your desires never fail in Jesus name.

Contents

Part IV: **Marriage Miracle**

Part V: **Ministers' Miracles**

Foreword

Healing is one of the greatest benefits that the Lord has given to His people and nothing stirs faith like the testimonies of people who have experienced our Lord's healing touch first hand. As a medical doctor, Tobe Momah deals with disease on a daily basis. He has a unique insight about illness and ministers the gifts of healing through various avenues. It is refreshing to have someone with a scientific mind validate the credibility of Scripture through real life human experiences.

Pastor Shane Warren
Lead Pastor
The Assembly West Monroe

Acknowledgements

God inspired this book. He gave the words and allowed me to put them in print. It, however, would not have been possible without some other invaluable assets along the journey who saw value in it and spurred me on.

More than anyone else, my wife of thirteen years, Rita Uchenna Momah, provided a setting that encouraged and sharpened me to write. She persisted and prodded me to continue, even when contending obligations nearly "froze" book-writing out of my busy schedule.

My church, the Assembly West Monroe, Louisiana, and my pastor, Shane Warren, inspired me to keep writing with their heartfelt worship, exceptional warmth and care, and the trail blazing word. These enabling surroundings helped the dream of this book become a reality. In fact, a member of the Church, Mrs. Burke, did most of the proof reading and corrections to the text and I am indebted to this Octogenerian for her help and support.

My parents General (Dr.) and Mrs. Momah continue to inspire me with their unconditional love and steadfast loyalty to family. They have supported my outlandish projects again and again and can be relied upon for untiring camaraderie whenever I need it. My brothers and sisters - Amaka, Ada, Emeka and Nkem - were all instrumental to this book's completion. I cannot over-emphasize the importance of theirs' and their families' help.

Finally, I want to thank supporters of my ministry-Faith and Power ministries-for their ardent support and steadfast loyalty. They spurred the publishing of this book with their fervent enthusiasm and spirit when I shared portions of it at our monthly Holy Ghost Night meetings or in correspondence. May what you have made happen in my life be multiplied many times in yours, in Jesus' name. Amen.

Introduction

This sequel to *Healing Lives* is an additional compendium of God's miraculous works in the lives of his people. It chronicles the ever-efficacious power in the blood of Jesus and corroborates the veracity of the scripture *"Jesus Christ the same yesterday, and to day, and for ever"* (Hebrews 13:8).

In an increasingly pantheistic, post-Christian and new age society, this collection of true stories authenticates God's healing power and manifestations in all facets of modern life. It delivers with simplicity the acts of God in individual's financial, marital, emotional, physical and spiritual situations with outstanding results.

Miracles, as catalogued in this book, are not a random, run-of-the mill, rudimentary or roll-of-the dice event that only happened thousands of years ago. They are daily supernatural events by a God of love who wants to show the world how much He cares about His people.

I hope as you read this book, it stirs your faith to believe God for your own miracle (John 19:35). It is *"...your Father's good pleasure to give you the kingdom"* (Luke 12:32) and His kingdom is not meat and drink *"...but righteousness, and peace, and joy in the Holy Ghost"* (Romans 14:17). Happy reading!

Tobe Momah, M.D.
West Monroe, Louisiana
December 2016

"And he that saw it bare record, and his record is true: and he knoweth that he saith truth, that ye might believe" (John 19:35).

PART I

My Personal Miracles

- Rita Momah: Attacking wrong attitudes by conquering depression!
- Delivered demoniac
- Saved from shame, a sexual pervert and syphilis
- The Girl who kept her baby
- Near death experience on the Delta
- Lori's miracle grandbaby
- Uncle Tony's supernatural recovery

When God visits you
it will be visible!

– Pastor Matthew Ashimolowo
(Senior Pastor Kingsway International Christian Center)

Chapter One

Rita Momah: Attacking wrong attitudes by conquering depression!

*"That the trial of your faith, being much more precious than of gold
that perisheth, though it be tried with fire, might be found unto praise
and honor and glory at the appearing of Jesus Christ: Whom having
not seen, ye love; in whom, though now ye see him not, yet believing,
ye rejoice with joy unspeakable and full of glory"* (1 Peter 1:7-8).

My wife, Rita Momah, is an invaluable asset and unquantifiable repository of goodwill to our marriage and ministry. She comes from a large home where she is the last born and was used to always having her way before we met and married. As marriage distilled in her, however, she began to understand Paul's assertion to couples in Ephesians 5:21 - *"Submitting yourselves one to another in the fear of God"* (Ephesians 5:21). She grew robust in the spirit and, academically, was stellar as she won awards at the masters' and doctoral levels in her public health graduate program.

She, however, was living through a grave misfortune. Having lost a baby in 2010, she was devastated. Future attempts at conception did not yield fruit, and my wife snowballed into depression in 2011. In those days, she drove three hours back and forth to school; and, at night instead of sleeping like someone who had just driven hours to and from school, she would be unable to sleep. She slept less than two to three hours a night and, in spite of our agreement prayers, she lost her zest for life and living.

Eventually, she broke the back of depression by meditating on the Word of God. She played Bible verses all day, meditated on the word of God and changed her pity party to praising God at every opportunity. She became involved with a Ladies female prison outreach ministry and joined the church choir at the Assembly, West Monroe, Louisiana. She also began to mentor young single females, volunteered in the kids Church, and gave *pro-bono* service at a pregnancy crisis center.

Priorities, pre-requisites and promotions!

Today, Rita is almost done with her doctoral degree program in public health. She has been inducted into the society for the highest academic achievements in her department, after passing her exams with stellar grades. All while still holding onto a fulltime job as a home health care executive. She refused to take the easy path to fame and fortune by immediately going into the job market after her Masters degree in public health, but has been patient and is now set for an academic career in the health sector.

She sleeps soundly and has never needed any psychotropic medications or undergone counseling throughout or after the ordeal. She is more ebullient in personality than ever before and has sown more baby showers in other to-be mothers than anyone else in the Monroe, Louisiana area. In the Holy Ghost meetings organized by the Faith and Power ministries, she supports my God given endeavors greatly, leads worship, maintains financial records astutely and handles all the logistics for our annual missions trips to Africa and Asia.

On numerous occasions, an innocent bystander has asked her *"how many children do you have."* To the aghast of her questioners, she would say confidently *"two, but they are yet to be born"* at which the questioner would gaze at her with marked suspicion of her mental coherence. She is, however, in excellent mental state and pursues diligently her vision of faith, family and fruitfulness in the kingdom of God without equivocation.

Life lesson 1: The power of God is the only power you need!

Don't run from your mountain; Speak to it and it will flee!

Chapter Two

Delivered Demoniac

"How God anointed Jesus of Nazareth with the Holy Ghost and with power: who went about doing good, and healing all that were oppressed of the devil; for God was with him" (Acts 10:38).

My wife and I were in a Sunday morning worship service when the unusual happened. As part of the medical support team in the church, my wife and I are usually detailed to the back of the church in order to respond quickly to any emergencies.

It was at that location that we noticed a middle-aged Caucasian woman walking around the back of the church gesticulating and speaking perversion into the atmosphere. While the rest of the congregation were lifting their hands or bending their knees in worship, this lady was gyrating back and forth under some external control.

As she came toward our seats at the medical support team desk, I called my wife and we began to bind and cast out the spirit of whoredom that was attempting to pollute the spirit of worship in the house. As we laid hands on this afflicted woman, she began to curse and say things that were incomprehensible.

My wife then laid hands on her belly and we decreed every evil spirit at work in her cast out. By this time a little crowd had gathered and suggested we move her out of the worship session to avoid distractions. I thought about it, but I decided against it knowing full well that a worship environment was actually the best atmosphere for her deliverance! As we continued to pray, binding and casting out any evil spirit attacking her, she fell out under the power of God.

Spirit of worship overcomes the spirit of whoredom!

When she arose, her visage was completely transformed. She told my wife and me that she had been under a satanic spell placed for years over her by evil associates and household enemies. Even though she had been coming to Church, she was still overcome by evil spirits repeatedly but now she declared she was free.

During these satanic attacks, she gets thoughts asking her to kill herself and even has intimate encounters with spirits in her dream. Since the prayers, however, she has been free from the rage and ravages of hell. She said, *"I have never felt freer and saner than after you prayed for me."*

I challenged her to give up any wayward habits that might be giving the enemy access to her life, and she invited my wife and me to pray over her home. After counselling her, she confessed that she had been watching horror movies and pornographic movies but was determined after that episode to jettison such habits.

Life Lesson 2: The name of Jesus is all you need to cast out a demon, no more no less!

*Yesterday is a bounced check,
tomorrow is a promissory
note and today is your
cash in hand – use it!*

Chapter Three

Saved from shame, a sexual pervert and syphilis

"...receive not the grace of God in vain. For he saith, I have heard thee in a time accepted, and in the day of salvation have I succoured thee: behold, now is the accepted time; behold, now is the day of salvation. Giving no offence in anything, that the ministry be not blamed..." (2 Corinthians 6:1-3).

A fifteen year old girl, alongside her mother, were in a physician's office for routine testing when it was discovered that this quintessential daughter and granddaughter of a famous local pastor, had been raped severally by her cousin's boyfriend. The incident only came to light because in the review of her laboratory work, it was discovered she had a sexually transmitted disease called syphilis which was impossible for someone who claimed to be a virgin.

On hearing the findings, this fifteen-year-old broke down in tears and sobbed continuously. She went to an all-Christian school and was an ardent church attendant at the church her grandfather served as pastor. Her family had no inkling on her predicament, and after counsel for the patient and comfort for the family, this fifteen year old innocent victim of an older sexual predator revealed how she had endured repetitive assaults at his hands for over a year.

Her life had gone from glory to shame as a result of these illicit, covert and traumatic sexual encounters perpetrated by this pedophile.

After the trauma, she was encouraged to look at herself as God sees her: a total treasure and not a heap of garbage as the enemy would want her to think. She was told again and again that Jesus loves her nonetheless of what happened, and, in conjunction with the family, security operatives were informed and the perpetrator identified, interviewed and prosecuted.

From corrupt to crucified with Christ

Two weeks later, after the unraveling of the incident, this fifteen year old's mother told physicians involved that the family were pressing charges against the villain, and wanted him fully prosecuted. Even though he was a partner to a cousin, and emotions were rife on both sides of the family, they wanted what was best for the victim and made a formal application to the district attorney for his arrest and trial.

This young girl, who had been molested, meanwhile re-ignited her passion for church and school again. She re-dedicated her life to Christ, and committed to steer clear of sex till married in God's eyes. She also lunged headlong into her academics, desiring a perfect SAT score for future placements in possible psychology and medical training.

Her sexual innocence may have been defiled, and her virginity damaged but, Jesus is the one for whom nothing is so damaged that He cannot restore. He has restored this darling of her family and school community to her once bubbly and cheery nature, and given her back the joy of her salvation without equal.

Life Lesson 3: God restores what man ruins!

God has the greatest leverage of all!

Chapter Four

The girl who kept her baby

"That our sons may be as plants grown up in their youth; that our daughters may be as corner stones, polished after the similitude of a palace: That our garners may be full, affording all manner of store: that our sheep may bring forth thousands and ten thousands in our streets" (Psalm 144:12-13).

My wife, Rita Momah, worked as the administrator of AFAM Medical Clinics in Brooklyn, New York between 2007 and 2010. On one occasion, a client of her medical office wanted help to abort her then ten-week-old fetus. Rather than show her the nearest abortificient or Gynecologist in her office who performed the procedure, my wife sat this formerly unknown woman down for hours asking her not to terminate her pregnancy.

After hours of pleading, cajoling and motivating, this woman agreed to save the life of her baby! She had asked for an abortion because of the poor relationship that had developed between her and the soon-to-be-born baby's father. She had struggled with her choice of abortion, but opted for it as a last resort to save the child from a life without a real family.

Eventually, this woman delivered a healthy baby boy at a nearby community hospital. She was a young, upbeat woman and about three months after the delivery, she was looking for a primary care provider to take care of her non-gynecological needs. She walked into the Family Medicine Clinic of Brooklyn Hospital Center, and as I walked in to see her, the first thing she noticed about me was my last name. She then asked matter-of-factly, *"Are you Rita Momah's husband?"*

Aftermath of an Avalanche

I answered, *"Yes, I am"* but quickly added *"Why do you ask?"* At that point, she told me about her chance encounter with my wife at her medical office a year ago and about how she had persuaded her to keep her newly-delivered bundle of joy. There, in front of me, was an African American woman and her baby as evidence of a woman's will to save lives even in a secular environment.

At that moment, I was never more proud to answer, *"Yes, she is my wife."* So I did! The emotions were overwhelming and we celebrated the tenacity and temperament of my wife to never give up on an ascribed objective. The patient then explained to me how the birth of her child had even helped heal wounds between her, the father of the baby and his family.

Today, that seed sown by my wife has matured into a young boy who walks the streets of Brooklyn without a care in the world. He is only one of many of my wife's fruitful efforts to save the unborn. As a volunteer at a crisis-pregnancy center in Monroe, Louisiana, she still advises young unwed mothers to save their babies.

Life Lesson 4: God is not mad at you; He is madly in love with you!

You can toil, but if there is no oil it will be foiled!

- Bishop Emmah Isong
(City of Testimonies, Calabar, Nigeria).

Chapter Five

Near-Death Experience
on the Delta

"...thy light break forth as the morning, and thine health shall spring forth speedily: and thy righteousness shall go before thee; the glory of the LORD shall be thy reward. Then shalt thou call, and the LORD shall answer; thou shalt cry, and he shall say, Here I am" (Isaiah 58:8-9).

On a flight from Louisiana to Maryland, in May 2016, I was sitting in my mid-row chair in the economy section of the plane when a sense of panic spread over the cabin area. I woke up to see an airhostess attempting to wake up a middle-aged African American male, but she was getting no response from him.

A plea was then made on the airplane's public-address system asking for any medical professionals on board to come to the front of the cabin section. I quickly stepped forward. An Emergency Medical Technologist who was on board was already standing over the comatose patient, with his now-hysterical wife literally beside herself next to him.

On a quick survey of the patient, I observed that the patient was diaphoretic, had labored respiration and was unaware of his surroundings. He had barely palpable pulses in his wrists and his blood pressure was markedly reduced. He had no history of heart disease or stroke, and was not on any medications currently.

One touch

As I laid my hands on this poorly responsive patient, I prayed under my breadth *"Lord, heal this man."*. The pilot was apprehensive of the worst and asked me if a possible diversion to the nearest airport was necessary. I told him, by faith, that the patient would be fine and that he should continue the journey.

I then stretched my hand to apply pressure on his sternum which is located on the anterior chest wall. After nearly three to five minutes of continual application on this gentleman's sternum, doing what medical professionals call the sternal rub, he finally opened his eyes and asked, *"Where am I?"*

He woke up without loss of verbal, physical or mental function. On arrival in Washington D.C, attendants whisked the patient off toward a waiting ambulance which he refused to board. He said that he felt fine, and would follow up with his personal physician. The family was profusely grateful for the help given to their husband and father, and Delta were so appreciative that they gave me a free airline voucher for any future trips.

Life Lesson 5: True Freedom is not doing what you want; it is doing what you ought.

It is not bragging
if you can back it up!

- Muhammad Ali (1942-2016)
(Three-time world heavyweight champion).

Chapter Six

Lori's Miracle Grandbaby

"...whosoever shall say unto this mountain, Be thou removed, and be thou cast into the sea; and shall not doubt in his heart, but shall believe that those things which he saith shall come to pass; he shall have whatsoever he saith" (Mark 11:23).

Mrs. Lori is an African-American member of the Assembly, West Monroe, Louisiana, and a patient of mine as well. On one occasion, she came to my office excited and glowing with joy. She told me about the prospect of her becoming a grandmother for the first time as her daughter who lived in Atlanta, Georgia, was going to have a baby boy in a few months.

A few weeks later she returned, but this time she was apprehensive and in tears. The baby, who was due to be born in a few weeks was doing well and so was her daughter. I could not understand therefore, the reason for her disturbed state of mind. It was then she unraveled her burdens to me.

The night before she came to the clinic, she had had a dream in which her daughter and grandson died in childbirth. Since that dream, she had been inconsolable. She was at her tether's end and had run to my office that morning believing I could speak a prophetic word that would cancel whatever evil premonitions the devil had for her daughter and yet-to-be-born grandson.

Full Term and flourishing

Right there in my office, I lifted up my voice and asked the God of heaven to deliver Lori's daughter and grandson from any untoward incident. I reassured Lori that her daughter and future grandson would be fine, and to rest assured in the promises of God for safety in childbirth.

In 2015, Mrs. Lori's daughter gave birth to a beautiful baby boy, without any incident. It was an uneventful delivery, and both Mother and son did well. Today, almost two years later Lori's daughter and grandson are in excellent health and are a witness of the power of the spoken word.

Lori's daughter is happily married, and she frequently dotes on her grandson when she babysits him. Her fears and night terrors were dismissed and the word of God established because of the word of faith spoken over her.

Life Lesson 6: Don't worry, but through prayer, be a warrior that wins all the time through faith!

You are the greatest prophet to your own life; so speak life!

Chapter Seven

Uncle Tony's supernatural recovery

"We have also a more sure word of prophecy; whereunto ye do well that ye take heed, as unto a light that shineth in a dark place, until the day dawn, and the day star arise in your hearts" (2 Peter 1:19).

D r. Tony is a Family Physician in Los Angeles, California. A successful father and husband, an entrepreneur and an esteemed son of Africa, he travelled to South Africa for an international conference in October 2014. While in South Africa, he fell mysteriously on the floor of the bathroom in his hotel room, and when he tried to get up, he could not move over half of his body.

Although Tony was partially paralyzed, he dragged himself to the telephone and contacted the front desk of the hotel. After initial evaluation by a local ambulance service, Dr. Tony was rushed to a South African hospital where was diagnosed with severe cervical spine stenosis. His nerves were paralyzed by the adjoining spinal cord and he required emergent surgery.

One word from God can change everything

Dr. Tony's family was aghast! He had always been the epitome of health and had never shown any signs of back pain or degenerative joint disease of the spine. His wife, Victoria, called me back after my initial efforts to reach her had failed and I told her the word of the Lord saying *Uncle Tony will make a full recovery.*

He was stabilized in South Africa and airlifted to Los Angeles Cedar Sinai hospital for emergency spinal decompression surgery. He successfully underwent surgery and continued for three months in the hospital undergoing physical therapy and back-strengthening exercises.

He was discharged in January 2015, and continued to exercise at home. He responded to therapy and was soon able to ambulate with assistance. By June 2015, he was back seeing patients in his office and by December 2016, he returned to Africa to collect an award.

He has made a full recovery, much to the surprise of all who saw him at the onset. He says about his upheaval, *"God gave me a second chance at life, and I will use this second chance to glorify God by lifting those around me."*

Life Lesson 7: Those who are failures in life are not those who fall, but those who fall and never get up again!

PART II

Money Miracles

- Restoration: The full package
- Awakened from the precipice
- One life to live
- Hyceinth Ahaneku: From woe to wonders
- Mrs. Jackson and house #117
- From drug dealer to deliverer from drugs
- John Belton: A meteor born with myositis
- Change in the midst of cerebral palsy
- Ms. K: From sex slave to sold out saint
- From rebel to righteous
- Ms. B: Blessed beyond measure

Until His vision for your life becomes your obsession, you cannot have it as a possession!

Chapter Eight

Restoration: The full package

"Wherefore He is able also to save them to the uttermost that come unto God by him, seeing he ever liveth to make intercession for them" (Hebrews 7:25).

Mr. G was torn apart spiritually, physically, emotionally, matrimonially and financially. Married to his second wife and still licking his wounds from a recent downsizing at work, he was faced with a home front that was disintegrating before his eyes.

His current wife had walked out on their marriage citing irreconcilable differences and his repeated affairs. Mr. G was in a state of utter disbelief. He had fourteen children by more than ten women and had been a well-known womanizer until recently when he met Christ while incarcerated for selling substances of abuse and child welfare defaults.

He had committed himself unconditionally to Christ, and with a promise to serve Him all the days of his life, joined a local Church on his release from jail. Mr. G suffered recurrently from diverticulitis, and other incurable diseases.

He sought out medical help, and as a signal to God's benevolence for him, the diverticulitis he had repeatedly been troubled with and the incurable disease he was said to have, disappeared and have not re-occurred since. His physical health improved, but his spiritual and financial health were in a state of unparalleled vortex.

Deliverance from pornography, Phencyclidine (PCP), gambling and deception

Unknown to anybody, Mr. G had a dark past. Apart from multiple affairs with countless women, that had taken its toll on his family, he was addicted to pornography, PCP and was a compulsive gambler. He watched pornography at the slightest impulse, smoked PCP daily, lied on instinct and was unable to obtain freedom from their cudgels.

On a certain Friday night, Mr. G went to a prayer meeting where, at the guest minister's invitation, he came forward and asked for prayers. Without being prompted, he told everyone within earshot that he wanted deliverance from pornography and PCP.

Immediately, believers prayed for him, hands were laid on him and anointing oil poured on him. He experienced instant freedom, and has not returned to pornography ever since. He is a constant attendant at church services, Sunday school teachings and today volunteers as one of the bus drivers in the church.

He worked two jobs at the onset of his release from jail, but today has a stable state job with benefits that affords him time to enjoy God's presence in church and small group sessions. He has also moved into a new four bedroom apartment, started dating a Christian woman he deeply loves and gives God all the glory for his supernatural turn-around.

Life lesson 8: Whatever God begins, He will end!

If satan has to seek whom he may devour, then there are those whom he cannot devour!

- Shane Warren
(Lead Pastor, The Assembly West Monroe Louisiana)

Chapter Nine

Awakened from the Precipice

"Therefore if any man be in Christ, he is a new creature: old things are passed away; behold, all things are become new. And all things are of God, who hath reconciled us to himself by Jesus Christ, and hath given to us the ministry of reconciliation" (2 Corinthians 5:17-18).

M
r. M had been a serial substance drug abuse user ever since he was twelve years old. Born into a Christian family, he fell out of regular church attendance following the break-up of his parent's marriage. Upset and disillusioned, he turned to marijuana, cocaine and heroine for relief.

He was arrested on several occasions for multiple misdemeanors bothering on theft, drug use and violent behavior. He lived a wayward life that was typified by use of sexual perversion, drugs and alcohol but he had a praying mother who never gave up on what God could do in her son.

In 2012, Mr. M was sentenced on a multi-count felony charge for selling drugs and aiding and abetting a drug dealer. He was placed in the isolation ward of the correctional center, and when he went to sleep that night he had a dream. He saw himself on the altar of a Church and the executive pastor appearing out of nowhere and telling him *"you know what to do."*

Miracle release, mechanical results, marital revival and motherly restoration

Mr. M woke up in cold sweat, and immediately called his mother. Their relationship had been strained by his drug use and repeated incarcerations, but he knew if there was one person who would understand the dream it was his mother. He told her about the dream he just had, and immediately requested that she bring his Bible to the prison. That day was December 30th, 2012.

He then told his mother that he wanted to surrender his life to Christ. The mother was ecstatic, and told a visiting Evangelist who was in town to go visit him in the prison in order to strengthen his faith. This evangelist saw Mr. M in the prison, and prayed with him. Mr. M covenanted to serve God in the ministry on release from prison, and asked for the Evangelist's oversight and tutelage.

Miraculously, Mr. M was released from jail earlier than his charge would have required. His sentence was shortened to less than two years, and he was released to his mother under probationary terms. He started attending Church and served as a minister to drug addicts in a rehab.

He also began working as an electrical mechanic with an engineering company and rose steadily on the job with excellent reviews from staff and customers. He has stayed drug free since release from jail, has had no probation queries and is currently engaged to be married to the girl of his dreams in 2017.

Life lesson 9: You can never be greater than your guide, or smarter than your surroundings!

The past is to be learned from but not lived in.

- Shane Warren
(Lead Pastor, The Assembly West Monroe Louisiana)

Chapter Ten

One life to live!

"Behold, I and the children whom the Lord hath given me are for signs and for wonders in Israel from the Lord of hosts, which dwelleth in mount Zion" (Isaiah 8:18).

Travon was a seventeen-year-old African American male with stellar grades who was about to graduate from high school. His mother had raised him in church, and I knew him as a firm believer in Jesus Christ.

He had endured a crossroad in his faith, especially after his older brother was diagnosed with cerebral palsy that left him without full cognitive function. Rather than be bitter toward God, however, Travon remained steadfast in faith and in fellowship.

His dad was part of his life; but in his mother's opinion he was not playing the role of a spiritual leader as well as he should. As a result, Travon had questions about his future career choices that he wanted to ask me.

From eerie to army!

Travon and his mother met me at a restaurant on a weekday evening after work to discuss his future career prospects. His mother was a teacher in elementary school, and she wanted him to blaze a trail in academics that would serve as a rallying point for his contemporaries. Her heart was set on Travon becoming a medical doctor, like me.

But Travon thought otherwise. Though good academically, he wanted to join the Military as a marine, and after a few years of military service then get sponsored by the military to medical school. His father was indecisive, and Travon wanted my opinion on this approach to getting into medical school.

I lauded his thoughtfulness and acceded to his proposal. I told him it was brilliant, but that it would require tenacious faith and unwavering belief to fulfill his dream of becoming a doctor. Two years later, Travon is a marine in the United States Military, and is deployed overseas to protect the territorial integrity of the United States.

Without any warning, Travon's mother died in January 2016 at forty-six years of age. He was devastated; he, nonetheless remembered his mother's drive and determination to help him become a physician and the need for him to be successful in order to care for his immediate family. He is pursuing his dreams with dogged faith and his life is witnessing incredible increase as a result.

Life Lesson 10: Life gives you back only what you put into it!

If you stand, after having done all to stand, you will not be standing very long!

- Kenneth Hagin Sr. (1903-1989)
(Pioneer Word of Faith preacher, and founder
Rhema Bible college, Tulsa, Oklahoma).

Chapter Eleven

Hycienth Ahaneku: From woe to wonders!

"And we know that all things work together for good to them that love God, to them who are the called according to his purpose" (Romans 8:28).

Hycienth Ahaneku is a prodigious young talent in the Nigerian medical field and its nascent Christian biosphere. He graduated in 2002 from the University of Nigeria Enugu Medical school, after having served as president of the Christian Union Campus Fellowship in 2001.

He exemplified humility, service to Christ and integrity as a campus Christian leader. In 2005, as a medical doctor post graduation, he re-located to the United States in pursuit of post-graduate training in Public health. His pursuits took him through the halls of elite American Ivory towers and culminated in the award of a Doctoral degree in Public health from the University of Texas, Houston, in 2013.

After the award of his doctoral degree, Hycainth worked as a post-doctoral fellow at the famed MD Anderson cancer Institute. In spite of his numerous achievements, Hycainth was not satisfied. He had applied severally throughout his ten-year sojourn in America for a medical residency but had repeatedly been turned down on countless occasions. He was, however, willing to try one more time!

Taught, Tolerated, Transferred and finally Tenured!

Hyceinth was instructing medical students and residents as a post-doctoral fellow at MD Anderson in 2015. More than anything else, however, he wanted to trade places with the residents. He had exhausted all his savings applying for residencies in the past and so, in 2015, he decided to apply one last time but to only one program this time.

He had been caricatured by relatives for not making any sustainable economic or financial impact in his community. After his residency application looked set for another disappointing season, and as pressure from his Nigerian home front intensified, Hyceinth took a job in Nigeria as a research analyst for a HIV/AIDS consortium. He maintained his high ethical standards and believed God for that miracle residency he truly wanted.

In March 2016, while working in Nigeria, Hyacinth received an email from the only hospital residency program he had applied to. The program told him he had been accepted as an internal medicine resident. He was ecstatic and lost for words except in awesome praise to the most-high God who made it possible. After more than ten years of waiting, Hyacinth's dream job finally arrived. Hallelujah

Life Lesson 11: There is no distance in the realm of the spirit.

It is your determination that determines divine destination!

Chapter Twelve

Mrs. Jackson and House No. 117

"And they that shall be of thee shall build the old waste places: thou shalt raise up the foundations of many generations; and thou shalt be called, The repairer of the breach, The restorer of paths to dwell in" (Isaiah 58:12).

Mrs. Jackson belongs to a rare breed of believers who stay with a vision until it becomes reality. Her tenacity and persistence were demonstrated no greater than in the establishment of Vision Academy, a charter school from grade six to twelve for boys and girls in Monroe, Louisiana.

Having worked as an English teacher in one of the busiest city schools, Mrs. Jackson established Vision academy to enable students with poor grades or dysfunctional homes an opportunity at quality education. She appeals to those students nobody else wants and so far over one hundred students have successfully graduated from Vision academy and gone on to higher education.

Amazingly, as a young woman Mrs. Jackson lived in an apartment complex right next to the site of her current school compound. Her family resided in apartment number 117, and she witnessed the ilk of inner city living. Her dream to one day own a school that would transform the mind and spirit of its students for Christ glory was framed in those early days, and in quest of a solution she proceeded to the University to study education.

After being hired by the city schools, and witnessing the myriad of societal ills in the public school system she desired to stem the tide of drugs, teenage pregnancy and violence that were plaguing Monroe and West Monroe's schools. She initially started with after-school classes in her garage, and later opted to start a new charter school to address these issues. She resigned her secure job with the city school board, and began a tortuous journey that would take her through nearly ten years of birth pangs before eventually Vision Academy was born.

Saving a generation

In 2001, Mrs. Jackson applied for a license to start a charter school in Monroe, Louisiana. A novel concept in Louisiana, it affords private individuals and organizations the opportunity to start schools that can be subsidized with government vouchers for their students. It, however, requires a lot of initial investment by the founders.

For nine years, the application for Vision academy was tossed back and forth. With no sustainable income or support base, Mrs. Jackson poured all her savings into the venture. She was unable to attract potential investors, and on one occasion while being interviewed by the local media told the reading public she needed a freehold property complete with basketball and sports complex to start the school.

Unknown to her a businessman who attended a certain Church in the city, and had never met her in person, read the interview and went to bed thinking about Mrs. Jackson's needs. In a dream that night, this business man heard God tell him to buy the seven acre property for Mrs. Jackson's school debt-free. He was to liaise with fellow Christian business men and banks that he had relationships with to raise the funds for Mrs. Jackson's project.

As it was customary with him, however, this businessman decided to discuss the investment with his wife. Without batting an eyelid, she concurred with his plans and he later testified that this was the first investment idea she agreed to immediately without delay!

As soon as this business man raised the funds, he contacted Mrs.

Jackson. She was in a state of utter shock, and acknowledged the business man's response as an answer to her prayers. She applied for the charter school license again, emphasizing the need to help disenfranchised students who were unwanted by the public school system. She tried to dispel the "messianic mantra" some had tagged her with, and offered to be a safety valve for students who couldn't succeed at regular schools.

In 2013, Mrs. Jackson's persistence paid off, and she was miraculously awarded the license to operate a charter school. The pastor of the Assembly, Shane Warren, and other believers in the area joined in prayer, mobilization and co-opting of students for the new school.

In her first year, she had more than twenty-five students and by the third year, the school had swelled to over one hundred students and twenty staff. Today, Mrs. Jackson has a state-of-the-art charter high school facility, and is expanding her frontiers. She plans, in 2017, to open two more charter schools in the Northern Louisiana area and knows that the God who did the first charter school will complete the others too!

Life Lesson 12: If it does not take from you, it will not stay with you!

You don't have anything to offer me but money!

- former McDonald manager in reply to a counter offer asking him to stay on instead of moving on to his vision for life.

Chapter Thirteen

From drug dealer to deliverer from drugs

"He raiseth up the poor out of the dust, and lifteth up the beggar from the dunghill, to set them among princes, and to make them inherit the throne of glory: for the pillars of the earth are the LORD's" (1 Samuel 2:8).

Mr. D was a drug dealer in a city in Louisiana. He trafficked and distributed nefarious drugs including cocaine, heroine, amphetamine and marijuana in that city and its surrounding towns. In the process, he became a purveyor of illicit drugs through which drug lords from other towns channeled their drugs into the city.

Though from an upscale family (Mr. D's father was a psychosocial therapist in South Louisiana), Mr. D had become depressed and sought solace in narcotics rather than regular anti-depressants or psychotropic medications. He descended downhill psychologically and sought solace more and more in substances of abuse like cocaine, heroine, amphetamine and marijuana. Eventually, he ended up sentenced to a Louisiana correctional prison for abuse and distribution of narcotics.

He served seven years in correctional prisons. While there he surrendered his life to Christ. He sought God's forgiveness, surrendered his life to Christ and soon became a leader in the local prison fellowship.

As a result of his stellar contributions in the prison, Mr. D was released earlier than the time of his scheduled sentence.

A Point of No Return!

Mr. D came out of prison in 2009, and joined a Church that re-connected him with his erstwhile prison companion called Mr. J. He began working odd jobs as a server in fast food restaurants, and while working at one of those jobs, met a lovely young lady called Ms. K.

She was a social worker, from an elitist background, and with an excellent Christian testimony. Even though Mr. D felt intimidated by her crystal-clear past, he felt encouraged by Mr. J's experience with his wife. Buoyed by his friend's experience, Mr. D asked Ms. K to marry him and she agreed. Today, they are a happily married couple with two beautiful boys born into it.

A few years after getting married, Mr. D was approached by a Christian business man and mentor to start a drug rehabilitation program for people suffering from addictions. This business man had sought a drug rehabilitation program in the area for a nephew, and when he failed to find one he decided to start one using Mr. D as his day-to-day operations guy!

He donated the facility, while Mr. D obtained the requisite documents. Ms. K used proceeds from her inheritance to also kick-start the project. Today that project is a cutting-edge drug rehabilitation center that provides a home for drug addicts in Louisiana from a Christ-centered perspective.

Life lesson 13: Some of those who finished strong started wrong but received God's healing prong along the way.

The devil only fights who he fears, not who men follow!

Chapter Fourteen

John Belton: A Meteor Born with Myositis

"But thou, Israel, art my servant, Jacob whom I have chosen, the seed of Abraham my friend. Thou whom I have taken from the ends of the earth, and called thee from the chief men thereof, and said unto thee, Thou art my servant; I have chosen thee, and not cast thee away. Fear thou not; for I am with thee: be not dismayed; for I am thy God: I will strengthen thee; yea, I will help thee; yea, I will uphold thee with the right hand of my righteousness" (Isaiah 41:8-10).

John Belton started in the backstreets of a little community in Louisiana, near Lake Charles. He developed Poliomyelitis early in life, and this made achieving his goals such as playing college football a daunting task. The medical experts told him he would never be able to play competitive college football because the braces he wore, as a result of poliomyelitis, would never allow him to run.

He refused to be deterred, however, and went on to play high school football. Eventually, in his senior year John played so well in his position he was voted the Louisiana all-state defensive most valuable player for 1981. As a result of his stellar football activity, he was drafted to play football for Mcneese State University Lake Charles, Louisiana.

Still faced with academic demagogues who felt he was not academically good enough to attend college, John proved another point. He went into Mcneese State University at the top of his class, and further cemented his academic credentials by graduating in

1986 with a Bachelor of Arts degree. He followed this achievement with a *Juris* Doctorate degree from Southern University, Baton Rouge, Louisiana in 1990.

District Attorney, Dad, Doctor of Marriages and Dragnet for business success!

John went on to marry Alana, a fellow persecutor, in 1991 and they have two children currently aged Twenty-two and Seventeen. Together, they built a law practice that spanned more than twelve thousand business, felony, misdemeanor and criminal convictions in the Northern part of the state of Louisiana.

They set up a marriage clinic for troubled marriages and organized marriage conferences that took them to different parts of the country. They also became advocates for abrogating the divorce process in Louisiana and helped the then governor promulgate a new law ensuring at least a year of separation before divorce becomes legal in Louisiana.

In 2014, John ran for District Attorney in the Union and Lincoln parish elections and won by less than a hundred votes. It was a testament to a life that had made a difference in secular and spiritual endeavors especially in northeastern part of Louisiana. Examples of his contributions include introducing a drug court for rehabilitation of drug addicts outside the prison in Ruston, Louisiana and serving on the boards of Southern University, Domestic Abuse Resistance Team (DART), Lincoln health systems foundation and the Eddie Robinson museum at the Grambling State University, Grambling, Louisiana.

He epitomizes a picturesque picture of decency in politics and family, especially in the African American community where single fathers have become a norm. He showcases the power of faith to overcome even the most difficult odds. The fight of faith is not just a cliché for John. It is a fact! Apart from his district attorney position, he lectures in Grambling State University as an adjunct professor of criminal Justice, and has made multi-million dollar investments in the real-estate and culinary business.

Life Lesson 14: Fear God alone or you will always fear something or someone less than Him!

Anywhere movement stops,
monuments are established!

Chapter Fifteen

Change in the midst of Cerebral Palsy

"And it shall be, when the LORD thy God shall have brought thee into the land which he sware unto thy fathers, to Abraham, to Isaac, and to Jacob, to give thee great and goodly cities, which thou buildedst not, and houses full of all good things, which thou filledst not, and wells digged, which thou diggedst not, vineyards and olive trees, which thou plantedst not; when thou shalt have eaten and be full" (Deuteronomy 6:10-11).

Amanda was born with cerebral palsy. As a result of her condition, she was unable to communicate or independently ambulate. Her mother made necessary arrangements for her to have twenty-four-hour care with the presence of support services.

In 2015, while her mother was taking care of Amanda in their rented home, a car drove into the compound and out of it came a well-dressed lady in a skirt suit. She introduced herself as a director of the company expanding the road on which Amanda and her mother lived.

The authorities had decided that some homes needed to be bulldozed for the new road being built to be finished. Unfortunately, Amanda's home was one of them. Because of Amanda's peculiar circumstances, however, the company had decided to relocate Amanda and her family for free!

New Beginnings

The company offered Amanda and her mom a brand-new-three-bedroom house with a back yard, fully paid for, in an upscale part of town. Included in the package were relocation costs, taxes and upgrades to make the new home compatible for someone with her disability.

Amanda's mom was astounded, but at the same time grateful to an all-knowing God who knew they needed more space for Amanda and her twenty-four-nursing care staff to utilize.

Three months later, Amanda and her family moved into their new fully furnished house with keys and title deeds in tow. She had gone from being a tenant to owning a property and land *et al.* God had metamorphosed her in twenty-four hours from a mere passerby to a proprietor of property by His favor.

This move has helped Amanda's health greatly. Her twenty-four-hour home health aides, who care for her round-the-clock, can now sleep in the guest room and still be readily available to care for her as the need arises. She is still physically disabled; but in her new stumping ground, she exudes the demeanor of the champion that she really is in Christ Jesus.

Life Lesson 15: If you work for everything you get in life, you will never live long enough to enjoy it!

You can't have satanic patrol, and expect divine overflow!

Chapter Sixteen

Ms. K: From Sex Slave to Sold-Out Saint!

"I will restore to you the years that the locust hath eaten, the cankerworm, and the caterpiller, and the palmerworm, my great army which I sent among you. And ye shall eat in plenty, and be satisfied, and praise the name of the LORD your God, that hath dealt wondrously with you: and my people shall never be ashamed" (Joel 2:25-26).

Ms. K at sixteen years of age had had more sexually transmitted diseases (STDs) than most adults would have had in a lifetime. In one year, as her supervising physician, I determined she had more than twelve (same or different) STDs. She always claimed, however, they were because of her promiscuous boyfriend.

On one occasion, I informed Ms. K's mother of her recurrent state of STDs. She brushed it aside blaming it on her daughter's misbehavior. On further enquiry of Ms. K, I learned she was not living with her parents but with a foster parent, who was nothing more than a concerned neighbor.

This concerned neighbor asked to speak to me privately on one occasion when one of several STDs was found in Ms. K's urine. She asked me to investigate if Ms. K's parents were managing her finances correctly, and if she were being used as an illicit sex object.

At that juncture, I invited Ms. K into my office and badgered her about her sexual promiscuity and any potential abuse from any quarter. She broke down in tears and in bitter anguish. At this juncture, I invited the Child Protective Services (CPS) to investigate the case and separated Ms. K from her biological parents by putting her in my office away from her parents.

Pimped, played but purified

Ms. K confessed to the CPS officers that she had been prostituting her body at the street corners of South Monroe, between classes. Her argument was that she had no clothes, toiletries or detergent and did what she did to augment her income. She also alleged that her parents took advantage of her financially, and when she requested assistance they always snubbed her.

As a last resort, according to Ms. K, she decided to hawk her body. She was so angry with her parents for collecting her monthly benefits but abandoning her financially. As a result of this disappointment, she felt she had to take her situation into her own hands.

A pimp in the area approached Ms. K and told her he would furnish her awash with clothes and toiletries if she would do his bidding. She was prostituting after school without the knowledge of her family or friends.

This act of pedophilia necessitated the immediate removal of Ms. K from her parents' home. She was taken into protective custody, while the police department sought out the pimp who hired her for money. Eventually, she was released from protective custody and placed in a foster home, where she was exposed once again to Christian principles and active church-going.

Today, Ms. K is about to graduate from high school. She hopes to pursue a business degree program in college. She works part-time to supplement her income, and has a strong Christian testimony. She hopes to become an entrepreneur and anything else God calls her to be.

Life Lesson 16: When a door opens, check behind it to see who opened it!

The world suffers from an identification, not identity, crises!

Chapter Eighteen

Ms. B: Blessed beyond measure

"...we have this treasure in earthen vessels, that the excellency of the power may be of God, and not of us. We are troubled on every side, yet not distressed; we are perplexed, but not in despair; Persecuted, but not forsaken; cast down, but not destroyed; Always bearing about in the body the dying of the Lord Jesus, that the life also of Jesus might be made manifest in our body" (2 Corinthians 4:7-10).

M s. B was born in New York City, USA in the middle of a protracted custody battle involving her parents and her siblings. This contention seared her throughout life, as her mother was pregnant with her while fleeing a manipulative and malevolent husband. Ms. B's mother re-located to the USA, with Ms. B's four other siblings, and a hiatus of an absentee father was instigated in their lives. This scenario persisted for the majority of Ms. B's life.

When she finally met her father, in her teens, he had re-married and had several step-children in addition to Ms. B and her siblings. He took her aside on one occasion and repeatedly scolded her for reading the Bible. He advised her to look to idolatry instead. What he did not know, however, was that Ms. B's emotions had been shattered not only by her parents divorce but also by a child predator in her family who had taken advantage of her innocence and repeatedly raped her.

The Bible was her only solace in those times of dark despondency, and Christ had become her only hope. Not getting much support from her biological father, she turned to friends but all to no avail. She was admitted to college but took a gap year abroad in Japan trying to get away from the sickening feeling that she had brought the sexual and emotional abuse on herself. Finally, everything caved in. Ms. B broke down emotionally and physically and had to be admitted to a tertiary care hospital for major depressive disorder with suicidal ideation.

From Faith to Faith

From depression, Ms. B went into severe anxiety and insomnia. She was re-located from the acute care hospital to a psychological rehabiliation center and advised by her team of Psychiatrists to get long-term psychotherapy alongside her current anti-depressant and psychotropic medications.

Her mother, while investigating options for her long-term therapy, noted a faith-based, female-only, Christian psychotherapy establishment. She approached them to take her daughter in, and even though the stipulations were onerous and places in the programs very competitive, they took Ms. B in for six months. They used faith-building and self-esteem boosting messages and physical rehabilitation as tools for equipping Ms. B to overcome the mood disorder that had weakened her resolve to live.

At the end of six months, Ms. B was a new person! She had reawakened her spiritual consciousness and was motivated enough to return to college in Georgia in pursuit of a nursing degree. She is sold out to Christ, and currently serves as a worker at her Atlanta-based Church. As a result of her inner healing, Ms. B is full of confidence about her future.

More than anything else, however, Ms. B is grateful she has a family again. Her once divided family is reunited with a new stepfather playing the role of a father figure. Though a Canadian by birth, and so not from Ms. B's ethnic group, this minister of the gospel and husband to Ms. B's mother has accepted Ms.B and her siblings as his own children. That assurance of a loving father, biologically and spiritually, has closed wounds that once seared Ms. B's heart.

Life Lesson 18: You either live by the Spirit or leave your calling because of the flesh.

PART III

Medical Miracles

- Delia Knox: Turning a twisted torso
- Ivo and Veronica's miracle baby
- Reinhard Bonnke and tales of the woman healed of cancer
- Way Nshe Bell: Healed by the Healer
- When lightning strikes twice
- Crandall: Cardiologist for Christ
- Melba: Raised from the ruins of a car wreck!
- Supernatural healing from brain tumor
- From mad hatter to made holy
- From infertile to fruitful
- The miracle man
- From depressed to dogged dominion
- Putting your best foot forward
- Deborah: Tasting the power of God
- Nonso and Cynthia: Let the healing streams flow
- Fabrice Muamba: Freedom from death
- From Mediocrity to meteoric rise
- Raised from the dead
- Called back from the dead
- Mr. R's revival after a round-robin life
- The Townsend's miracle baby
- Dr Drumgole's miracle grandchildren
- Marie Smith: From near death to new beginnings

- Liberated from Leukemia
- The Youngs' everlasting joy
- Restoration, revival and renewal
- From malignant to miracle
- From Zero to hero (heart)
- Austin Parsley: From Asperger's to astounding
- Jean Neil: Healed from the head to the heels

Nobody is good enough
to be your enemy

- Dr. Uma Ukpai
(Uma Ukpai Evangelistic association, Uyo, Nigeria)

Chapter Nineteen

Delia Knox: Turning a twisted torso

"And these signs shall follow them that believe; In my name shall they cast out devils; they shall speak with new tongues; They shall take up serpents; and if they drink any deadly thing, it shall not hurt them; they shall lay hands on the sick, and they shall recover" (Mark 16:17-18).

On Christmas day in 1987, a drunk driver in Toronto, Canada, hit Delia. She was in the car with her twin sister, brother-in-law and their children and even though there was no loss of life, Delia was left paraplegic in her lower extremities as a result. The drunk driver was arrested and jailed, but Delia was left bound to a wheel chair for the rest of her life.

She continued to serve God faithfully and every day she woke up, she believed God for her healing. She met her future husband-to-be - Bishop Levy Knox - at a Charismatic Christian conference in 1996, and by 1997 they had gotten married. She led the music and arts department of the Church, characteristically leading worship in her wheel chair, while her husband served as the senior Pastor.

Even though wheelchair bound, she continued to lead worship at the Living Word Christian Church in Mobile, Alabama, USA. She was highly acclaimed in the music ministry, and received accolades from secular and gospel artistes including Shirley Caesar with whom she even did a duet.

In August, 2010 Bishop Knox called Pastor John Kilpatrick of the

Church of His Presence, Mobile, Alabama and told him, *"I want to put my face in the window of the revival sweeping through your Church in the ongoing Bay revival."* He attended on August 27, 2010, with his wife, first lady Delia Knox, and their lives have never been the same since.

By fire, force and faith!

At the Bay revival on that fateful day, with a worldwide television audience watching, Evangelist Nathan Morris and Pastor John Kilpatrick prayed for Delia Knox. She felt a surge of electricity go through her formerly paralyzed and insensitive lower extremities, and screamed to Pastor John and Evangelist Nathan that something was happening to her formerly insensitive lower limbs.

She had prayed, and been prayed for, several times by others but with no evidence of healing. This time, however, it was different! She could feel her husband's hands on her legs and heard the voice of the Holy Spirit tell her, *"Arise and walk."*

As she stood for the first time in twenty-two and a half years, she wobbled but chose to slug on. Her husband and Pastor Kilpatrick held her on both sides and assisted her as she tried to ambulate with her lower extremities for the first time in decades. Eventually, after thirty minutes of intense congregational prayer and praise, she began to work independent of her two assistants. She went to bed that night thinking she was dreaming, but woke up the next morning aware that she was really healed.

She stood on the pulpit of the Bay Revival venue subsequently, and testified to a worldwide audience of her healing. Six months thereafter, she went to upstate New York to visit her parents after a fifteen-year absence. For the first time, she was able to climb the stairs leading up to her parents' house unaided. At the reception filmed by the secular media, the mayor and city council acknowledged her miracle as what only God could have done and, as a result, conferred her and her husband with a key to the city and a plaque of notable achievements in the history of their town.

Life Lesson 19: Whom man calls an invalid, God calls invaluable!

You may not know what tomorrow holds, but you know the one who holds tomorrow!

Chapter Twenty

Ivo and Veronica's
Miracle Baby

*"Then many of the Jews which came to Mary, and had seen the
things which Jesus did, believed on him"* (John 11:45).

Ivo and Veronica Drazenovic are family physicians in Brooklyn,
New York who graduated from the Brooklyn Family Medicine
residency program in 2009 and 2011 respectively. They first met
in Venezuela, and married post medical school in Venezuela, before
choosing to relocate to the United States of America (USA) in 2005.

Before arriving the USA, however, they had a son who was in his
early teen years when the parents were in residency. During their
years of residency, the Drazenovics' desired another child, but they
were unable to conceive. It was at this same period in time that Ivo
noticed a hard and painless swelling in his left testicle.

In 2007, after evaluation and diagnosis by an expert urologist,
Ivo was diagnosed with testicular cancer. He underwent removal of
the left testicle (orchiectomy) and chemotherapy successfully. He,
however, according to oncologic opinion had a greatly reduced chance
of ever procreating or having a child with his wife as a result of the
surgery.

Recovery, revival and results

The Drazenovics continued in their secular life with dogged contentment and a pursuit of excellence. Their teenage son grew, graduated from high school and got admitted to one of the elite colleges in Brooklyn. The parents had, meanwhile, become faculty and directing staff at a nearby community hospital and were considered role models in the immigrant community as a result of their stellar family and ethical values.

Eighteen years after her last pregnancy, and at the age of forty, Veronica Drazenovic became pregnant again. She felt unusually nauseous one morning, and because she knew she had not had a regular menstrual period for more than six months, she decided to do a pregnancy test. To her utter shock, she discovered she was pregnant.

In March 2016, Veronica gave birth to a beautiful baby girl in an uneventful vaginal delivery. Their family was finally complete, with Ivo, Veronica, their son and now their precious baby girl. The Drazenovics' are enjoying more than ever the exciting clime of Brooklyn. Even though medicine told them they would never have another family member, God over ruled man's opinion and today their miracle baby lives.

Life Lesson 20: What God does is forever, but what man does is only for a moment.

Chapter Twenty-one

Reinhard Bonnke and
tales of the Woman
healed from Cancer

*You can move from
probable to possible when
faith in God is applied!*

Chapter Twenty-one

Reinhard Bonnke and tales of the Woman healed from Cancer

"I sent my word, and it healed them and delivered them from their destructions" (Psalm 105:17).

R einhard Bonnke was ministering in Soweto, South Africa, when he received a note at an Apostolic Faith Mission (AFM) Conference asking him to come to the bedside of a member of the church in Pretoria, South Africa, to pray for her healing. She had been diagnosed with terminal cancer, and the doctors had given up on her.

Evangelist Bonnke hesitated initially, but under the conviction of the Holy Spirit he decided to go and pray for her the next day. She lived in an affluent neighborhood in Pretoria, South Africa, and he was concerned that the apartheid government's policy on racism would not allow his co-workers who were Black Africans come alongside him to pray for this dying woman.

As a missionary with the AFM, Reinhard had been preaching across racial barriers in then apartheid South Africa, and not a few feathers in the AFM church were being ruffled. He had established the Lesotho AFM church, and alongside his assistants had given correspondence

Bible college classes to thousands in Maseru, Lesotho, and seen several afflicted Africans saved, healed and filled with the Holy Ghost.

As they approached her house, a member of the church the lady attended told Reinhard, *"I have no problem with black persons, but they may not want to see a black person in their home."* He directed his complaints towards Michael Kolisang, an African and a local of Soweto, who had accompanied Reinhard to this upscale suburb of Pretoria, South Africa.

Renewal of Strength

Disgusted by the culture the Church in apartheid South Africa had embraced, but nonetheless obedient to God's call, Evangelist Reinhard asked Michael Kolisang, his assistant, to wait outside while he prayed for this wealthy lady. As they walked into the lady's bedroom, Reinhard Bonnke perceived the presence of the spirit of death in the room.

The lady was lying in bed and writhing in pain, but as soon as Reinhard entered the room, her countenance brightened like a light bulb on a Christmas tree. To the chagrin of her fellow church member and some members of her family, she asked *"where is Michael Kolisang?"* When Reinhard explained his whereabouts, she immediately asked him to go bring in and let them both pray for her.

When they returned, Evangelist Bonnke read a scripture from Habakkuk 3:17-19 for this dying lady. As he finished quoting the passage, which speaks about rejoicing no-matter-what and walking on one's high places, this lady broke down in tears and wept. She said that God had told her that He wanted her to walk on her high places! In fact, prior to Reinhard Bonnke's arrival, she had been reading a book titled *Hind's Feet on High Places.*

They (Michael and Reinhard) now prayed for her, and as soon as they finished she noticed a refreshing like a waterfall come over her. A week later she went to the Cancer Research Institute; after a battery of tests, not one trace of cancer could be found in her. She was totally healed of cancer. She went on to live another thirty to forty years and throughout her life remained an avid supporter of Christ for All Nations (CFaN), the umbrella organization Reinhard Bonnke founded.

Life lesson 21: Signs and wonders follow those who are following, and are faithful, to God's word in their lives.

If Christ took away our sickness and diseases, then it is not possible to have them if we are in Christ!

Chapter Twenty-two

Way Nshe Bell:
Healed by the Healer

"Men do not despise a thief, if he steal to satisfy his soul when he is hungry; But if he be found, he shall restore sevenfold; he shall give all the substance of his house" (Proverbs 6:30-31).

Way Nshe Bell has been happily married to her husband, Mr. Bell, for more than ten years at the time of this writing and together they have three lovely children. They married when Way Nshe was twenty-one years old and her husband was Twenty-two years old.

During her first pregnancy at the age of twenty-three, Way Nshe's physicians noticed she had a rapidly deteriorating renal function and called her attention to it. Prior to that, Way Nshe had been the epitome of good health. She attended an apostolic Church in Monroe, Louisiana, and was an ardent worshipper of God and follower of Jesus Christ. Her family, friends and fellowship members were shocked at the sudden malfunction of her kidneys, but no one was more shocked than Way Nshe herself.

After the successful delivery of her first child, Way Nshe underwent a kidney biopsy that revealed the source of her renal insufficiency. She had nephrotic syndrome and was immediately placed on corticosteroids and chemotherapy to stem the tide of nephritis invading her kidneys.

Her condition, however, continued to worsen; and, eventually, in 2012, Way Nshe was placed on hemodialysis.

Pregnancies, parenting and peritoneal dialysis

Way Nshe continued a thrice-a-week rigorous hemodialysis schedule while taking care of her ailing mother-in-law, and raising a family which included two additional children both delivered while she was on hemodialysis. She was also a dutiful wife to her hard-working husband, who was now the sole bread winner for the family, as Way Nshe had to relinquish her job at a prestigious bank to care for herself and her family.

Throughout the ordeal of hemodialysis, however, Way Nshe never allowed the pain of her condition nor the pressure points in her home defeat her or douse her optimism. She recalls, during those days, just telling herself over and over again "this must be done" and then just doing it!

She never shrunk from going to church, and continued to lead prayers and praise sessions in her local Church. After her third pregnancy, Way Nshe decided to change the way she did dialysis. In order to spend more time with family and watch her children grow, she opted for peritoneal dialysis, a procedure done by the patient in the confines of their bedroom thrice a week and which afforded her that kind of opportunity. This continued for two years.

In January 2015, Way Nshe received a call from Little Rock, Arkansas, about a possible kidney match for her. The donor was a teenager who had died instantly in a motor vehicle accident. After only eleven months on the kidney transplant list, Way Nshe was to be the recipient of his harvested kidneys.

She had the kidneys transplanted, and returned to normal health in record time without suffering any repercussions from the procedure. She no longer needs dialysis, and has developed a *bona fide* compassion out of her experience for others fighting such ailments. As a result, Way She is today a patients' advocate fighting for the cause of the forgotten and frustrated with little or no hope in our world today.

Life Lesson 22: Nobody can stop a man or woman who chooses to believe in his or her God!

**You can't soar and be
sour at the same time!**

Chapter Twenty-three

When Lightning Strikes Twice!

"I shall not die, but live, and declare the works of the Lord*"* (Psalm 118:17).

M s. L is a Fifty-year-old African American who has lived with the human immunodeficiency virus (HIV) for nearly thirty years. She was seen in 2012 for a left-sided-facial rash that covered nearly ninety per cent of her left eyelid. It was diagnosed eventually as ophthalmic herpes zoster. On subsequent work-up, it was discovered that Ms. L was HIV positive.

Apparently, Ms. L was in denial about her HIV status. She had been diagnosed at a prenatal facility in Los Angeles, California, in 1987, but she refused to take antiretroviral medications because of their potential harm to her unborn son. After the birth of her son, however, Ms. L carried the virus asymptomatically for upward of twenty years until that fateful day it was re-discovered in 2012.

She went on to start antiretroviral treatment and was faithfully complying with her treatment when lightning struck a second time. About four and a half years after the initial ophthalmic herpes zoster was treated with anti-viral eye drops, Ms. L presented again with left eye photophobia (bright lights) and impending blindness. She could not look into any light source, had crusting around her left eye and was in exquisite pain.

This is not my Portion!

After initial evaluation and treatment, Ms. L was admitted to the floor of a nearby community hospital for worsening facial and abdominal pain. She was evaluated by numerous surgeons and physicians who diagnosed her with herpes zoster (ophthalmic) and severe colitis.

The prognosis they gave Ms. L, however, was abysmal. They portrayed doom and gloom and treated her as though she was already at death's door. Ms. L was, however, not ready to die. She woke up one morning and challenged the *status-quo*.

A Bible-believing and Spirit-filled Christian, Ms. L began to quote to herself the scriptures that pertained to long life. She refused to believe the negative reports of the medical personnel. Within three days, she was discharged in a fully-functional state.

After that spell of near-death, Ms. L was given a government subsidized and newly furnished house in her community. Her eyesight has miraculously improved and her abdominal pain is stable. She reminds everyone who cares to hear that *"death and life are in the power of the tongue and they that love it shall eat the fruit thereof"* (Proverbs 18:21). Ms. L chose life and today her life is an evidence of it.

Life Lesson 23: You cannot conquer what you fail to confront!

*Faith is a decision,
not a deliberation!*

Chapter Twenty-four

Crandall:
Cardiologist for Christ

"Then he answered and spake unto me, saying, This is the word of the Lord unto Zerubbabel, saying, Not by might, nor by power, but by my spirit, saith the Lord of hosts. Who art thou, O great mountain? before Zerubbabel thou shalt become a plain..." (Zechariah 4:6-7).

D r. Chauncey Crandall is an outstanding cardiologist in Palm Beach, Florida who has been in medical practice for more than twenty years. He speaks regularly in Christian outreaches testifying about the outstanding miracles God has performed in the course of his clinical practice.

One healing miracle that stands out for Dr. Crandall, however, is the story of Jeff Markin who was brought unconscious into a local Florida hospital emergency room in November 2003. He was pronounced dead on arrival (DOA), and after one hour of failed resuscitation he was pronounced dead by the medical team.

The emergency room physicians then paged Dr. Crandall and he confirmed Jeff was actually dead. As he turned to leave the exam room where Jeff's body was lying lifeless, he heard the voice of the Holy Spirit tell him, *"Turn around and pray for that man again."*

Acceptable Time of Salvation

The average brain does not survive more than five minutes without oxygen. Even if a person survives, this lack of oxygen causes anoxic encephalopathy and results in residual lifelong neurologic deficits. To Dr. Crandall's medical mind, it was foolhardy to attempt to pray for Jeff as he was already dead. Even if he were raised from the dead, he would have irreversible neurological damages as a result or so he thought.

Before he could voice his protestation to God, however, he started blurting out a prayer over Jeff saying, "*Father God, I cry out for this man's soul; and if he does not know you as Lord and Savior, raise this man from the dead.*" To the consternation of the rest of the medical staff, Dr. Crandall requested they shock Jeff one more time.

They had already shocked him repeatedly but because Dr. Crandall requested it they decided to do it, albeit reluctantly. Immediately they shocked him with the defibrillators, his former "flat-line" EKG came to life with a regular heartbeat. The room erupted in spontaneous awe and Jeff woke up with his crying daughter holding his hand.

To confirm the miracle even further, Jeff was certified as having no neurologic deficits. While dead, he recalls being in the middle of his funeral service when a certain person called Bob appeared to him and told him he had to go back. He believes that Bob was his guardian angel and that God brought him back from the dead in order to give him another chance.

Life Lesson 24: Fear tolerated is faith contaminated!

The highways of God are the highways of success!

- Dr. Uma Ukpai (Uma Ukpai Evangelstic Association, Uyo, Akwa Ibom Nigeria)

Chapter Twenty-five

Melba: Raised from the ruins of a car wreck!

"Many are the afflictions of the righteous: but the LORD delivereth him out of them all. He keepeth all his bones: not one of them is broken" (Psalm 34:19-20).

Melba is an ardent believer living in Monroe, Louisiana. A passionate worshipper of Jesus, she served as a home health aide assisting clients in their homes and demonstrating the love of God to them. She is happily married to her husband of fifteen years, versatile as an usher and Bible study leader in her local Assemblies of God church and, through the fear of the Lord, raised three daughters in the power of the Holy Spirit.

She had multiple medical problems but was in otherwise stable health when, driving home on a fateful day, she lost control of the steering wheel and was hit by another car. She went headlong into a ditch, lost consciousness, was airlifted to a tertiary health center and did not recognize anyone until 48hours later.

She had multiple facial fractures, bilateral leg fractures, and generalized skin lacerations. Her condition was dire, and as a result, the nearby community hospital she was sent to initially stabilized her, but immediately referred her to the Level one trauma center closest to Monroe, Louisiana.

Tried, trusted and true

On arrival at the trauma center, Melba underwent multiple surgeries and spent upwards of fifty days in the hospital undergoing rehabilitation and multiple skin graft and orthopedic surgeries. She had stage 3 generalized skin burns and, according to one of the nurses who admitted her, she was praying to God when she was brought in.

During her time in the hospital, she came face to face with doubt and depression. She questioned her faith, snapped easily at loved ones and wallowed in self-pity. She looked a shadow of herself with the scars and bruises blighting her otherwise beautiful face and body.

On discharge, she had to temporarily move from her house into her daughter's place as a result of an unprecedented flood in the Monroe, Louisiana area. Melba, however, remained undaunted. She recovered her faith and love for the Lord and chose instead to concentrate on the positives and ignore the negative things around her.

Today, Melba is back in her home, with her husband and children. She has fefained full function physically and spiritually. She refuses to feel sorry for herself, but instead goes to church, participates actively in caring for her children and grandchildren and ministers in any capacity she can when afforded the opportunity. She has learnt through her ordeals to follow God into whatever area He chooses to lead her into, knowing God will always come true to his word.

Life Lesson 25: Though bones may break, and many may moan, a true follower of Jesus Christ never lives alone!

If the value of something is based on what someone will pay for it, then you and I must re-evaluate our worth (in Christ).

- Shane Warren
(Lead Pastor, The Assembly West Monroe La)

Chapter Twenty-Six

Supernatural healing from brain tumor

*"Who his own self bare our sins in his own body on the tree,
that we, being dead to sins, should live unto righteousness:
by whose stripes ye were healed"* (1 Peter 2:24).

P aisley Hatfield was less than a year old when her parents noticed a deviation on her left side with inability to close the left eyelid. They took Paisley to her local pediatrician who requested a Computed Tomography (CT) scan of the Brain without contrast.

After the CT scan at Cincinnati Children's hospital, her pediatrician informed the parents that little Paisley - who was less than 3 months old at the time - had a tumor on the base of her brain. It would require immediate biopsy and possible explorative surgery by a pediatric neurosurgeon.

The parents were flabbergasted and overwhelmed. They never expected their little angel to have a tumor. As Christians, they prayed and committed the procedure into God's hands. On the day of the procedure, several friends, family and church members were praying for Paisley when an astounding discovery was made.

Turnaround breakthrough!

On that fateful Monday, November 24, 2015, Paisley underwent the procedure. When the neurosurgeon came out, he was baffled and shaking his head. He told Paisley's puzzled parents, *"Your prayers must have worked, because when I went in to get that biopsy, nothing was there."*

The hospital released a statement corroborating the neurosurgeon's findings. They said *"Doctors at Children's had expected the worst - a malignant tumor. But when surgeons reached the spot where the suspected tumor was visible on the scan, they found nothing. They couldn't have been happier to tell the good news to the Hatfield family[1]."*

Six months later, Paisley is clinically stable with no sign of any neurological damage or recurrence of the facial palsy that triggered her work-up in the first place. Her parents, Matt and Carissa Hatfield, tell the world, *"It's a true miracle, it's a true healing."* They are witnesses to the miraculous and the divine intervention that was, and is still, medically inexplicable.

Life lesson 26: Amazing is God's address!

---

[1] Hill Prudence. Doctors go to biopsy baby's fatal brain tumor and they can't believe what they see. *International Journal Review*. November 2015.

If you ignore the Word of God, you introduce the rod of the wicked into your life!

Chapter Twenty-seven

From Mad hatter to made holy

"Wherefore I put thee in remembrance that thou stir up the gift of God, which is in thee by the putting on of my hands. For God hath not given us the spirit of fear; but of power, and of love, and of a sound mind" (2 Timothy 1:7).

I was teaching Sunday School at my church one fateful Sunday morning when my Pastor's armor bearer interrupted me, and asked me to see him immediately for an emergency in his office. A member of the church, Ms. D, had displayed abnormal scenes in the morning service. After much prayer, my pastor had brought her to his office and wanted some medical advice.

I left the Sunday school class and met, in my pastor's office, a middle-aged Caucasian woman in a state of panic, frenzy and utter chaos. After discussing with my pastor and listening to the heart cry of her family, I prayed for her and advised her husband to bring her to my office as soon as possible.

The husband then lamented to me that his wife, who used to be a high-level sales woman for a national electronics brand, had not slept for seven days straight and was impossible to live with at that point. Turning to me, he said, *"I will do whatever you want me to do to make her recover her normal mind."*

From glory to glory

The following week I saw Ms. D in my office. Again, I spoke to her as gently as I could, reassuring her of my best intentions. I could see she was out of sorts and in a highly agitated and confused state.

I instructed her husband concerning what I wanted him to do, in terms of adjusting her prescriptions. I ordered some laboratory tests and recommended psychological support for which D and her husband gladly obliged. They made an appointment with an in-house psychologist, and though the following twelve months were tenuous, by the grace of God, Mrs. D made a slow recovery.

She attends church and Sunday school regularly, sleeps adequate number of hours and is able to function as a wife and business partner for her husband. Her speech that was once pressured and erratic is now calm and measured. She had made such vast improvement that even her counselors, friends and family testify that it could have been only through the finger of God, not man's, that she improved so much.

Her Psychologist told me in confidence that her turnaround is the most phenomenal change he has ever witnessed and only God could have done it. She has stabilized physically and mentally and regained her ability to interact socially with her peers. Most important of all, however, is the fact she loves the Lord Jesus Christ and her family and friends more than ever and will not do anything to harm that relationship.

Life Lesson 27: One minute with God is better than a mile walked with men!

"If they have been wrong before, it is more than likely they will be wrong again"

- Pastor Shane Warren (The Assembly West Monroe La)
(referring to medical treatise on Ashley Miller's pregnancy)

Chapter Twenty-eight

From infertile to fruitful

*"Lo, children are an heritage of the Lord: and the fruit
of the womb is his reward"* (Psalm 127:3).

T he Helps pastor at the Assembly, West Monroe, Louisiana Pastor Christopher Miller and his wife Ashley, were told by reproductive endocrinologists they could never have children. They had tried to have children for five years without success, and decided to seek contemporary medical opinion. They said Ashley's reproductive system would never be able to carry a baby and advised them to adopt or to forget about ever having children.

In 2014, Rita Momah (my wife) and Pastor Christopher were speaking about the medical report that Ashley had received. My wife, while believing God for our own children, agreed to join Pastor Christopher in prayer to reject that medical report. They prayed for each other in faith notwithstanding their negative medical reports.

Pastor Christopher later, while reminiscing on the prophecies over his life, recalled how in February 2010 Pastor Shane Warren had told him and another couple to expect children soon. The other couple manifested within a year by giving birth to twins but five years later Christopher and Ashley's miracle baby was still being awaited.

The birth of Elijah

Without Assisted Reproductive Therapy (ART), Ashley Miller suddenly discovered she was pregnant in February 2015. She went to the same doctor who told her she would never have children. He told her she was pregnant but that the fetus would not survive. They explained to her that the fetus was an unviable embryo, and that she should prepare for premature abortion.

Heart-broken and disconsolate, Ashley and Christopher told their Senior Pastor (Shane Warren) what the medical experts had just said. In reply, he told them, *If they had been wrong the first time, it is more than likely they will be wrong again!* That Wednesday, at the weekly mid-week service, prayers were made for the yet-unborn Elijah. The Miller family went home strengthened, and believed God for the life of their little angel.

Pastor Shane was right! The medical experts were wrong once again. That "unviable" embryo survived, and nine months later a beautiful baby boy called Elijah was born. Today, little Elijah is the cynosure of all eyes as a testimony of the power of God. His life has "*...turned wise men backward, and maketh their knowledge foolish;... (and)...confirmed the word of his servant, and performed the counsel of his messengers*" (Isaiah 44:25-26).

Life lesson 28: You can argue with explanations, but you can't argue with evidence!

If you don't quit, you can't lose!

Chapter Twenty-nine

The miracle man

"He suffered no man to do them wrong: yea, he reproved kings for their sakes; Saying, Touch not mine anointed, and do my prophets no harm" (Psalm 105:14-15).

Minister Cletus is an ardent worshipper of God. He serves at the Assembly, South Monroe, Louisiana as a minister and in the prison with Set Free Prison Ministries. In 2014, he noticed that his eyes were deeply jaundiced (or yellow), and he was losing weight rapidly. He easily became tired, lost all appetite, and was increasingly looking malnourished.

Medical studies done at a nearby tertiary hospital diagnosed Cletus with Hepatitis C, and in his current state, was told he was in the last stages of hepatic encephalopathy or chronic deterioration of the liver. The prognosis was poor, and a life expectancy of six months was given to him. He went home dejected and without any hope.

He lay at home, seemingly to die, but fervent prayer was made for him by the saints. In a space of days, Cletus sister drove down from Houston, Texas and evacuated him to a liver center especially dedicated to such conditions. He underwent laboratory and radiological studies, and after this a therapeutic intervention that transformed his liver was made.

Nothing wrong with your liver!

At this foremost liver center in Houston, Texas, Cletus's laboratory and radiological findings returned within normal limits. Barely a month after he had been discharged from the hospital in Monroe, Louisiana, with failing liver levels and what looked like a cancer ravaged liver, all his studies were normal again. The only abnormality noted on the battery of tests was Gastro Esophageal Reflux Disease (GERD).

Miraculously, without any medicine or surgical intervention Cletus liver was restored. Even though he still carried a positive serology for Hepatitis C, the liver enzymes were within normal limits, and his work up did not show any presence of cancer in his body.

Six months after his discharge for a seemingly-terminal condition, Cletus returned to Monroe, Louisiana, in perfect health. He regained his weight, is looking well-nourished, and is even more ardent in his service to God. His testimony has drawn several people to Jesus Christ. The experience has grown him in both spiritual and physical stature. Today, he works as a counselor and mentor to a group of men who are undergoing substance abuse rehabilitation. He is bearing fruits in the ministry, as God restores his health.

Life Lesson 29: Stop living in the realm of probabilities, and enjoy the era of all possibilities in God!

It is okay when a child is afraid of the dark but it is a tragedy when a grown man is afraid of the light!

- Ancient Chinese Proverb

Chapter Thirty

From depressed to dogged dominion!

"But ye shall be named the Priests of the LORD: men shall call you the Ministers of our God: ye shall eat the riches of the Gentiles, and in their glory shall ye boast yourselves. For your shame ye shall have double; and for confusion they shall rejoice in their portion: therefore in their land they shall possess the double: everlasting joy shall be unto them" (Isaiah 61:6-7).

Mrs. J and her husband were two of the first people to welcome my wife and me into their home in West Monroe, Louisiana. They poured unconditional love and exposed us to intimate southern hospitality at the Assembly, West Monroe and even afforded their house as a rest pad anytime we needed it.

Their son, who was more of our contemporary, developed a bond with my wife and me and God blessed our relationship spiritually, socially and in secular endeavors. Mrs. J had been a nurse before retirement, and in the church served as the leader of the medical support team.

She is a virtuous woman, filled with the spirit of God who had raised her children and grandchildren in the fear of the Lord. In her past, however, were dark secrets she had never shared with anyone but which were about to be unraveled.

The voice from another world

On a fateful Sunday service in 2012, one of Mrs. J's grandsons walked up to the platform and confessed to having thoughts of suicide. Prior to that, the pastor had released a word of knowledge about someone who came to Church with the intention of hurting himself afterward.

This incident served as a wake-up call of sorts for Mrs. J. She reminisced on her childhood and noted the domineering influence of depression on her father, brother, herself and now her grandson. She had personally suffered with Major Depressive Disorder (MDD) for years, and even though she was still able to function as a nurse, she was irritable, listless and would spend her Sundays, when she was not working, crying in her bedroom instead of going to church. At a point, she actually wanted to end her life as a result of the devil's assault on her mind.

She had kept this secret for too long. Now this enemy was pillaging her heritage as well. She vowed enough was enough! She delved into the word of God and chose to create her world based on God's design for her life. She discovered truth from God's word such as *"the Kingdom of God is righteousness, peace and joy in the Holy Ghost"* (Romans 14:17), and that depression was not part of God's package for her life. Immediately, she made these discoveries, Mrs. J was set free from MDD.

She stood in front of the church, on a Sunday morning, and openly testified of God's hand of healing and recovery that brought her from depression to dominion. It was a word from a heavenly world, not man's word, that transformed her life. Today, Mrs. J and her family are leaving a life free from the shackles of MDD.

Life Lesson 30: Every tragedy starts with F.E.A.R (False Evidence Appearing Real).

When heaven backs you, you can never be at the back no matter who barks at you!

**- Pastor Matthew Ashimolowo
(Kingsway International Christian Center,
London, United Kingdom).**

Chapter Thirty-one

Putting your best foot forward

*"The steps of a good man are ordered by the Lord: and
he delighteth in his way"* (Psalm 37:23).

Mrs. May is a pharmacist and member of the choir in her local church. She had suffered for years from a "pinched nerve" condition in her back. After due work-up, and being diagnosed with spinal stenosis she underwent - on the advise of her Neurosurgeon - spine surgery to correct this condition.

Unfortunately for her, however, a major nerve that supplied sensation to her right leg was damaged during the surgery. On recovery, Mrs. May discovered that she was unable to elevate her right foot upward. Instead of moving above the ground when lifted, the right foot flapped on the ground.

This unfortunate episode continued for three months. As a result, Mrs. May was forced to move about with a cane and to take time off work. The surgeon offered her physical Therapy and asked her to hope for a possible restoration of the nerve connection as it was almost impossible for surgery to restore the damaged nerve.

Reconnection after a disconnect!

Mrs. May got depressed, despondent and drained of spiritual power as a result. A faithful worshiper of God, she felt robbed of her dance and praise to God by her physical condition. She was in church one Sunday when God spoke to her to "get internally healed so that her external health can manifest."

Immediately, she repented of her moodiness and the spirit of heaviness that had beleaguered her spiritual condition. She then asked for divine reconnection beyond the ability medicine offered. She stood in faith with the Church prayer team, and asked for a full restoration of the damaged nerve.

The power of God overwhelmed her, and within a few weeks her hitherto flapping right foot was moving in the right direction. She returned to the choir, more determined to serve God fully, and put her best foot forward in kingdom service! Although, she still undergoes physical and occupational therapy, she has since returned to work and is a testimony of God's help even when medicine falls short.

Life Lesson 31: Men care, but God cures; Men help, but only God heals!

*God is not going to get even
with you because Jesus
is your eventuality!*

Chapter Thirty-two

Deborah: Tasting the power of God

"For it is impossible for those who were once enlightened, and have tasted of the heavenly gift, and were made partakers of the Holy Ghost, And have tasted the good word of God, and the powers of the world to come" (Hebrews 6:4-5).

F ew people taste the power of God in an overwhelming manner during their lifetime, but Deborah did. She had been hospitalized after a motor vehicle accident that left her back and hip in pain. After a week of persistent weakness, associated with nausea and vomiting, her sister rushed her to a local hospital for emergency attention.

After twenty-four hours of treatment, during which time Deborah became progressively worse, doctors at her local hospital transferred to a larger community based hospital where more specialist services were available. On arrival, Deborah was already unconscious and non-responsive to verbal commands.

Her sister who had accompanied her to the hospital is a member of our prayer ministry in Monroe. On arrival at the hospital, she called my wife and told her about Deborah's dire condition. Rita, my wife, got there just before she was intubated and wheeled off to the Intensive Care Unit (ICU) of the hospital and was able to minister to her in prayer.

Miracles made-in-heaven

In the ICU, a septic work-up revealed that Deborah had a valvular vegetation that was spurting out bacteria. As a result, she had developed bacterial meningitis. Medical personnel placed her on intravenous antibiotics; and after a few days, surgeons performed an open heart surgery to remove the defective valve and replace it with a bioprosthetic heart valve.

The condition was called endocarditis, and according to the physicians taking care of her, she was alive only by Divine Providence. She eventually turned the corner, after spending more than thirty days in the hospital, and ended her sojourn in the hospital undergoing cardiac rehab for another thirty days.

Ms. Deborah followed her hospital stay with a nursing home admission. Since leaving the nursing home, she has been fully functional and has no residual deficits. She is an evidence of the power of prayer, and a strong sense of community amongst the church. No wonder the Bible adjures believers to *"...pray one for another, that ye may be healed. The effectual fervent prayer of a righteous man* (or woman) *availeth much"* (James 5:16-18).

Life Lesson 32: Those who learn from history do not repeat history, but they make history instead!

*The Lord God never makes
the pathway to greater
blessings enviable!*

- Shane Warren
(Lead Pastor the Assembly West Monroe, Louisiana)

Chapter Thirty-three

Nonso and Cynthia: Let the healing streams flow

"...every thing that liveth, which moveth, whithersoever the rivers shall come, shall live: and there shall be a very great multitude of fish, because these waters shall come thither: for they shall be healed; and everything shall live whither the river cometh" (Ezekiel 47:9).

In October 2013, after nine months of married life, Nonso and Cynthia were ecstatic to discover that Cynthia was expecting their first child. It was a Saturday, and as they settled into a night of celebration and camaraderie with other Nigerians in the Monroe, Louisiana, area Cynthia noticed something flowing down her legs.

She ran to the bathroom and as soon as she sat on the toilet seat, she expelled a dead fetus. In tears, she called her husband and informed him of what had just happened. He took her to the nearest hospital where their worst fears were confirmed: Cynthia had just had a complete abortion. Her obstetrician recommended serial monitoring of her pregnancy hormone levels as an outpatient.

Both Nonso and Cynthia were devastated, but they continued to trust God for a turnaround of their fortunes. Six months later, Cynthia discovered that she was pregnant again. She went to her obstetrician, and after a pelvic ultrasound doctors informed the couple that Cynthia had an ectopic pregnancy that was infiltrating the walls of the fallopian tubes and that the fetus needed to be expelled by abortificient injections.

After the injections, however, there was evidence some damage had been done to the fallopian tubes. The Obstetrician ruled, based on a hysterosaplingogram, that Cynthia had a less than ten percent chance of conceiving in the future. They advised them to pursue Assisted Reproductive techniques (ART) instead, and referred them to a near by reproductive endocrinologist.

From Barren to blessed

As Nonso took his wife home, in the silence of the car, he ruminated about what the Obstetrician just said. She had predicted they would have a life without natural conception of children. The couple, however, knew what God had promised them and this information was against the promises of God. They decided, there and then, to believe God's report while exploring any scientific advances that could improve Cynthia's fecundity.

After seeing the reproductive endocrinologist, Cynthia was placed on fertility-enhancing medications as she continued her studies as an undergraduate student. In April 2014, she became nauseous and on further evaluation was found to be carrying twin daughters. Cynthia was a wonder beyond words to her medical community. It was a supernatural act of God Almighty and as an acknowledgement, they decided to name the girls *Amarachuckwu* meaning Grace of God and *Ogochukwu* meaning the favor of God.

At thirty-six weeks of conception, Cynthia's water broke and she was rushed to the hospital. On arrival she underwent emergency Cesarean section and delivered two beautiful bouncing baby girls. Today, those girls are the quintessential expression of beauty and power in one. They are a product of the hand of God, and as stated in the Holy Scriptures are "...*wonderfully and fearfully made*" (Psalm 139:14). As for Cynthia, she is still having children, notwithstanding the evil medical prophecy of barrenness the devil tried to sell to her. To God be the glory!

Life Lesson 33: Few go down the halls of faith where great rewards lie!

All your prayers are working people thank you so much. To God be the glory!

- **Shauna Magunda,** (then fiancée of Fabrice Muamba, on twitter the day after he died for 78 minutes).

Chapter Thirty-four

Fabrice Muamba:
Freedom from death

"...according to his own purpose and grace, which was given us in Christ Jesus before the world began, But is now made manifest by the appearing of our Saviour Jesus Christ, who hath abolished death, and hath brought life and immortality to light through the gospel" (2 Timothy 1:9-10).

F abrice is a Congolese immigrant who moved to the United Kingdom in 1999, at the age of Eleven, as a result of his family's persecution by the Congolese authorities. After arriving in England, he attended an elementary school in Walthamstow, near London, England, and began pursuing a career in football by enlisting with the Arsenal academy.

At the age of Seventeen, Fabrice turned professional and played for Arsenal in the football league cup. He moved to Birmingham city football club in 2007 and played seventy games for them. Eventually, he signed on at Bolton Wanderers in 2008 and played for the England under-21 team as a defensive midfielder.

While playing for Bolton Wanderers football club on Saturday, March 17, 2012 in a match with Tottenham Spurs Football club for the qualification into the semi-finals of the FA Cup, Fabrice collapsed and became unresponsive. The medical team rushed toward him, and for seventy-eight minutes tried to resuscitate him without success.

Turn around breakthrough

Fabrice was taken by the Emergency Medical services to the London Chest hospital and, en route the hospital, he received more than fifteen automatic emergency defibrillation shocks. He had been treated by the team doctors of both teams, and a spectator in the crowd who happened to be a consultant cardiologist with the National Health services of the United Kingdom.

His team mates and the crowd at the White hart stadium feared the worst, and abandoned the game while the scores were 1-1. The fiancée, and Fabrice's chauffer – Curtis Codrington-, however, kept vigil at his hospital bedside praying and believing God for his speedy recovery. After seventy-eight minutes of no heart beat, Fabrice's heartbeat returned and within seventy-two hours, he opened his eyes and his first words were in French asking about the welfare of his three-year old son, Joshua.

To his medical care team, Fabrice's recovery was nothing short of a miracle. The brain does not survive more than thirty seconds without oxygenated blood but in his case, his cognition remained intact. After the incident, Fabrice retired from professional football in August 2012, married his fiancée at a ceremony in October 2012, obtained a bachelor's degree with honors in July 2015 and is currently studying for his masters' degree in sports journalism.

Today, Fabrice and Shauna have two children of their own – Joshua and Matthew - and Fabrice is working part-time with ITV, London as a sports commentator. He has authored a book titled, *I am still standing* and Shauna has started a confectionary line showcasing her savory Caribbean sauces called *Mrs. Muamba's sauces*. In addition, Fabrice has lent his vocals to a collaboration of celebrities who composed a single titled, *Wake me up*, for *Children in need* - an international charity - in November 2014. The song went to the top of the charts in the UK and raised millions of pounds for charity.

Life lesson 34: The bigger the enemy comes, the harder he falls before a believer!

We owed a debt we could not pay, and so Jesus paid the debt He did not owe!

Chapter Thirty-Five

From Mediocrity to Meteoric rise

"And the spirit of the LORD shall rest upon him, the spirit of wisdom and understanding, the spirit of counsel and might, the spirit of knowledge and of the fear of the LORD; And shall make him of quick understanding in the fear of the LORD..." (Isaiah 11:2).

A aron was born with a metabolic abnormality that caused him to absorb heavy metals abnormally. His medical condition required him to have a delayed educational pathway that required special educational classes for him. As a result, he did not graduate from high school with his contemporaries.

Although, he was an introvert, he was very investigative by nature and began exploring peoples' ancestry through online material. Not satisfied with just ancestry investigation, Aaron enrolled for a full degree program at the School of Urban Missions (SUM) West Monroe, Louisiana.

His family were apprehensive, and cautioned him not to raise his expectations especially in terms of academics. Aaron has, however, defied those odds and has re-defined excellence in life and ministry. He participates fully in academics, social and spiritual activities and is one of the best students in his class currently.

In pursuit of excellence

Now in his second year of Bible school, Aaron is a much sought after thinker and speaker at student events. He still needs a scribe to copy his notes and his mother to cook select meals for him, due to his dietary peculiarities, but otherwise Aaron is pursuing excellence with dedication.

He has refused to let his medical condition, heavy metal disease, deter him. He is determined to attain the high mark of God's calling for his life, notwithstanding the odds. Aaron has determined in his heart, like Daniel did in Daniel 1:8, to move barriers no matter what they are and to become who God has called him to.

He is passionate about defending the vulnerable and the defenseless, as a result of the behavior meted out to him in his growing years. He has trail-blazed a peculiar path in his Bible school – School of Urban Missions - and engineered a spirit of possibility in people with life-long diseases and disability.

Life Lesson 35: A job is what you are paid for, but your call is what you are made for!

Pain lasts a moment; Quitting lasts forever so push through it!

- Bishop Hanchey
(Power Chapel International, Monroe, Louisiana, USA)

Chapter Thirty-Six

Raised from the dead

"By faith Abraham, when he was tried, offered up Isaac: and he that had received the promises offered up his only begotten son, of whom it was said, that in Isaac shall thy seed be called: Accounting that God was able to raise him up, even from the dead; from whence also he received him in a figure" (Hebrews 11:17-19).

At seventeen years of age, Seth Hanchey was the youth pastor of Power Chapel International (PCI) Monroe, Louisiana. He is the only son of Bishop and Pastor (Mrs.) Hanchey who are the founders of PCI. He was, and still is, an avid runner. In celebration of his high school graduation, he committed to doing the Ironman Triathlon.

As he prepared for this epic day, he rode his power bicycle on the streets of Ruston, his home town. On September 28, 2011, as he rode his bike, he was rear-ended by an elderly grandmother. Before she could stop the car, however, she had knocked Seth over one hundred feet into a guard rail which caused a complete distortion of his facial anatomy.

Seth was airlifted to Louisiana State University (LSU) hospital in Shreveport, Louisiana and diagnosed with complicated traumatic brain injury. He had several skull and spine fractures and had lost complete function of his right side. He underwent multiple surgeries, and was told by the specialists at LSU Shreveport that *"He came as close to death as you can without going."*

The dreamer never dies regardless of the outcome of his dream

The doctors' verdict concerning Seth was a poor prognosis. They said he would never walk or talk again, and at best Seth would be a vegetable with no quality of life. Bishop Hanchey and his wife, were however determined to defy those odds.

The hospital was, according to Bishop Hanchey, his Mount Moriah and the Bishop was determined not to leave that mountain without his "Isaac." Alongside Seth, the Bishop had a long history of cycling up and down the hills of Ruston and this was the time to go up the mountain of healing together!

Seth inspired the nurses on his ward by his dogged determination, and they nicknamed him *Ironman* as a result. Within six months, Seth had started texting and writing *yes* or *no* on scraps of paper. In the last five years, he has regained independent mobility and speech.

He pulled through the pain barrier, and today he is rehearsing for the Ironman Triathlon on the same bicycle he was riding when the grandmother's car hit him. He has also started a foundation for traumatic brain injury sufferers called Team Seth foundation, through which he hopes to give a voice to those who, otherwise, would be voiceless.

Life lesson 36: Too many fail at the edge of their breakthrough because they quit too soon!

I have the power to take your life, but I do not have the authority!

- God's reply to Evangelist Jesse Duplantis
when enquiring for long life.

Chapter Thirty-Seven

Called back from the land of the dead

"See now that I, even I, am he, and there is no god with me: I kill, and I make alive; I wound, and I heal: neither is there any that can deliver out of my hand" (Deuteronomy 32:39).

Mrs. Green was in the hospital for infection-induced sepsis. She had suffered from cholestasis of the biliary tree and had undergone a cholangiogram and subsequent cholecystostomy in a nearby community hospital. Rather than get better, however, she had gotten only worse.

While in the hospital Intensive Care Unit, in 2013, she asked the family to put a call through to my wife and me. She had, according to her family, seen my wife and me in a vision praying for her and was convinced that if we prayed for her she would be healed.

My wife was unavailable, but I headed to the hospital on that eventful day. Seeing her emaciated and jaundiced in the hospital bed, I could sense the spirit of death hovering around her. She was unresponsive and unaware of my presence; but, notwithstanding, I closed the door, cried out to God on her behalf and anointed her with oil according to James 5:16.

A life turning miracle

Within twenty-four hours, Mrs. Green was responsive again and full of energy. A life that had been paralyzed, pain-wracked and pauperized through sickness was suddenly changed. God had begun a quick work in her, and even her family and medical personnel were shocked at her speedy recovery.

Seven days later, Mrs. Green was released from the hospital and sent to a local nursing home. She hosted my wife on the nursing-home grounds several times and remained ebullient and full of life. She used a wheelchair to get around, but though her physical body was constrained her spirit was never limited.

Until her death in 2015, Mrs. Green was full of vitality and energy. From the nursing home, she sent supportive words and prayer to Rita and me and supported our ministry in several diverse ways. Mrs. Green is a testimony of the power of prayer to break sickness.

Life Lesson 37: Be careful what you say because it will come to pass.

The worst enemy of the
best is the good!

Chapter Thirty-Eight

Mr. R's revival after living a round-robin life!

"And David came to Baalperazim, and David smote them there, and said, The Lord hath broken forth upon mine enemies before me, as the breach of waters. Therefore he called the name of that place Baalperazim" (2 Samuel 5:20).

M r. R is currently in his mid-thirties; he has lived through a life scarred by multiple childhood traumatic experiences. He suffered repeated rejections as a child, and grew up ridiculed by his friends and foes alike for his untoward family background.

At the age of three, his mother shot his father to death right in front of he and his older sister. As a result of this capital offence, Mr. R's mother was sentenced to life imprisonment by the courts.

Her children were taken in by his paternal grandparents and as Mr. R grew into his teenage years, he delved into drugs, sex and alcohol. In 1998, he suffered a major trauma to the brain that left his brain scarred, and eventually culminated in daily seizures which were uncontrollable even on medications.

Twenty-Four-hour miracle

The consequence of this spate of repeated seizures was impeded educational and occupational attainments that threatened his overall well-being and livelihood. For ten years, Mr. R went from neurologist to neurosurgeon and yet the seizures became worse.

After fourteen years of incarceration, Mr. R's mother was released from jail and she invited Mr. R to her Church. At the age of Twenty-five years, and at the end of himself, Mr. R attended a Church service and at the end of the service, he surrendered his life to God.

The pastor and the youth pastor laid hands on Mr. R and decreed the end of epilepsy in his life. After the service, Mr. R went back to the medical professionals supervising his health, and on repeat examination the scar noticed on prior brain scans had disappeared.

Even more noteworthy, however, was the fact that Mr. R has not had a seizure since 2007, when he surrendered his life to Christ. He has continued as a member of the Church, gotten married, is the father of a three-year-old son and works in an international retail company as an internal auditor.

Life Lesson 38: It is not over until God says it is over!

Amazing is God's address!

Chapter Thirty-Nine

The Townsend's Miracle Baby

"He sent his word, and healed them, and delivered them
from their destructions" (Psalm 107:20).

P astor Townsend is a virtuous woman of God who has inspired
hundreds of women in the Monroe/West Monroe area of
Louisiana with her cutting edge ministry and excellent
preaching. She has planted several churches, served on the board
of several not-for-profit organizations and has been instrumental in
birthing revival in the twin-city area.

Pastor (Mrs). Townsend has also been happily married to her
husband for more than thirty-five years, and they have a son.
Unfortunately, this son and his wife, who have been married for more
than ten years, had no children. Expert opinion had been sought,
but without any success. Instead they grew discouraged and became
emotionally, financially and spiritually drained as a result.

Knowing the mood of despondency their son and his wife were
in, Pastor Townsend invited them to a meeting she was hosting in
West Monroe, Louisiana, with Evangelist Jerry Mcgee. The couple,
meanwhile, had become used to going to gospel crusades and being
prayed for with nothing changing.

Fulfilled till Overflowing

Pastor Townsend's daughter-in-law was sitting akimbo in the service when Evangelist Mcgee called her out for special prayers. He told her she would have a child within twelve months. As she laid his hands on her she passed out on the floor.

Her mother-in-law was shocked because she had never told the visiting minister of her son and his wife's travails. Her son watched his wife gather herself from the floor. Then, they held each other hoping and believing God for a miracle.

A month later, the daughter-in-law was pregnant with a beautiful baby girl. The doctors could not explain it, except to say it was a miracle. It was the finger of God without a doubt!

Nine months later, the couple had a beautiful baby girl born to them. This singular incident sparked faith in the hearts of the younger Townsend couple. Today they serve in the ministry alongside their parents. Hallelujah

Life Lesson 39: Impossible doesn't exist when God is present!

Those who fight the good fight of faith never lose in the battles of life!

Chapter Forty

Dr. Drumgole's miracle grandchildren

"...blessed is she that believed: for there shall be a performance of those things which were told her from the Lord" (Luke 11:45).

T he senior pastors of Liberty Christian Center, Monroe, Louisiana, Dr. and Mrs. Drumgole have an erudite and peerless son and daughter-in-law who are devoted followers of Christ. They had been married for six years and were childless. The Gynecologists had told Mrs. Drumgole, the daughter-in-law of Dr. Drumgole, that she could not have a child due to the proliferative fibroids in her womb.

In 2013, they were getting used to not being able to have a child and were ready to settle into life as a childless couple. They were already in their late thirties, and did not think God would still visit them. It was then, however, that their faith was stirred by a prophetic declaration. The visiting minister called them out in a meeting and declared the word of God over them. He told them, *"Twins would be born to you in twelve months."*

They were shocked at the prophecy, but it was corroborated by Dr. Drumgole who said it would not just be twins but a boy and a girl child born to the couple. In twelve months, in confirmation of prophesy, the twins were born. Even though medical opinion had been increasingly pessimistic about the feasibility of Dr Drumgole's daughter-in-law's pregnancy, considering she was thirty-eight years old, the pregnancy was uneventful and the twins born in superb health.

Another surprise

Twenty-eight months later, the Drumgole family awakened to another surprise. Their daughter-in-law, who was once called barren, was pregnant again! This time the baby was a boy, and even though she would be forty-two years old at delivery, she believed God for a miracle childbirth.

In June 2016, she delivered a bouncing baby boy to the ecstasy of her family and with glory and praise to God. She and her husband, after that baby was born, decided to get a surgical procedure to – in their words - ensure God had no more surprises in store for them.

Their miracle children have inspired other couples with similar problems to believe God for their own performance in His time. The Drumgoles' continue to serve God as workers in the layman ministry and share their testimony readily in different church forums. Like Elizabeth, Mrs. Drumgole has become a lightning rod for other couples' believing God for the fruit of the womb.

Life Lesson 40: No prophetic word goes without divine performance!

Silence in the face of evil is itself evil: God will not hold us guiltless. Not to speak is to speak. Not to act is to act!

- Bonhoeffer, Dietrich (1906-1945).

Chapter Forty-one

Marie Smith: From near death to new beginnings!

"the heart of this people is waxed gross, and their ears are dull of hearing, and their eyes have they closed; lest they should see with their eyes, and hear with their ears, and understand with their heart, and should be converted, and I should heal them" (Acts 28:27).

Marie is a warrior for the Lord. Currently in her late seventies, she has been a Christian for almost fifty years and has lived out her life with faith and fervor. A member of the local apostolic church, Ms. Marie is looked up to as a mother in the church and has trained up several ministers, including her son who is the district presbyter for the Monroe, Louisiana area.

In 2015, however, she was diagnosed with Renal Cell Carcinoma, a disease with a life expectancy of less than three years. With surgical exploration and excision, however, life expectancy could be extended to five years. Marie was already a hemodialysis patient and considered in poor health for such a major surgery but she was nonetheless unperturbed by the negative medical diagnosis and uncertain prognosis.

She chose to undergo surgery, trusting that God had a plan for her life beyond three years. She remained resolute and confident in God's ability to bring her through, and after the requisite cardiac and pulmonary clearances were obtained, Marie had the surgery, albeit with complications.

Postoperative Complications and Praise's Creativeness!

After being given anesthesia and undergoing a three-hour surgery to remove her right kidney, the anesthesiologist alerted the surgeon to Ms. Marie's hypoxemic and hypotensive state in the operating room. She had no verifiable heartbeat, and her blood pressure was plummeting rapidly. The surgical team immediately started cardiac resuscitation and called in the cardiologists on call.

When all attempts to awaken Ms. Smith failed, the surgeon left the operating room to tell her son who was outside the operating room that his mother was dead. Ms. Marie's son, the presbyter of the local apostolic church, on hearing the news became distraught and started crying with his head in his hands.

His sister who was next to him rejected the doctor's report, however, and rebuked her brother sharply saying *"You are the pastor; stop crying and start praying."* They lifted up their voices in unison and asked God to revive Ms. Smith. As the surgeon returned to the operating room, he was shocked to hear Ms. Smith heartbeat had returned.

The cardiologists kept her in the hospital for three days, during which they were monitoring her for any complications of prolonged hypoxemia. Ms. Marie had been anoxic for upwards of ten minutes, but to the specialists' surprise, she recovered without any deficits.

She confounded all medical opinions proposed about hypoxemic postoperative complications and repeatedly told anyone who cared to hear, *"it was not yet time for her to go to heaven."* She continues to travel extensively sharing her testimony of being raised from the dead and continues to give God all the glory for her resurrection from the dead.

Life Lesson 41: Follow God and He will cause signs and wonders to follow you!

*God seeks worshippers,
not worship!*

Chapter Forty-Two

Liberated from Leukemia

"...Jesus saith unto them, Yea; have ye never read, Out of the mouth of babes and sucklings thou hast perfected praise?" (Matthew 21:16).

Ms. T was only Eight years old when her parents noticed bilateral neck swellings which were increasing in prominence. As pastors and missionaries in America, they committed their oldest daughter to God's hands and claimed God's promises over her.

Unfortunately, she only became worse. Unable to attend school, Ms. T developed high-grade fever that was associated with nose bleeding and excruciating bone pain. After discussing the condition with her Pediatrician in California, they were referred to a Pediatric Oncologist who opted to do a bone-marrow biopsy.

The biopsy confirmed the clinicians worst fears. Ms. T had acute lymphocytic leukemia in an advanced stage. Her only remedy at that juncture was chemotherapy which would mean financial expenditures way above their budget and more missed days from school.

Free at last

Ms. T started chemotherapy and within three months she was clear of all cancer cells. She did not suffer any side effects such as nausea, hair loss or malaise as other chemotherapy patients had. To her team of clinicians, she was a miracle.

She testified that she won the battle over leukemia on her knees and by praising God, notwithstanding her circumstances. She remembers singing praises to God and receiving a definite touch that she believes was a confirmation of her healing.

To all and sundry, Ms. Tis a miracle. She corrects anyone who tries to give medicine the credit, that God - not medicine - healed her. Today, she is a pre-med student at a tertiary medical institution in the United States of America. She is determined to share her testimony of God's supernatural wonder working power by relating her story to similarly medically-afflicted individuals she encounters.

Life Lesson 42: If God does not set you free, you can't be Free Indeed!

When the immoveable meets the unstoppable, the lesser power must bow.

Chapter Forty-three

The Youngs' Everlasting Joy

"Sing, O barren, thou that didst not bear; break forth into singing, and cry aloud, thou that didst not travail with child: for more are the children of the desolate than the children of the married wife, saith the Lord" (ISAIAH 54:1).

Mr. and Mrs. Young got married, in their late thirties, at a nearby Monroe, Louisiana, Baptist Church. My wife and I were invited to the wedding because as advocates for godly marriage, we had told the couple that *"marriage is honorable in all, and the bed undefiled: but whoremongers and adulterers God will judge"* (Hebrews 13:4).

The gentle prodding my wife and I gave them encouraged them to walk down the aisle and get married, two years after they started living together. Five years after the marriage, however, they had no children. Mrs. Young already had a son, from an earlier relationship, but Mr. Young had never had any children biologically.

To make a bad situation even worse, Mr. Young lost his job with a leading bank. After first being unemployed, he later became underemployed by his own standards. To cut costs, Mr. and Mrs. Young moved in with Mrs. Young's mother, but this arrangement only made them perpetually sullen and sorrowful.

Nobody but God!

Mrs. Young, meanwhile, was depressed by her inability to conceive. She had a phenomenal sixteen-year-old son but she wanted a child with her new husband as well. They began attending the Assembly, West Monroe, Louisiana desiring change in their spiritual, secular and spurts of ill-health that had made her unable to conceive.

The Gynecologist had told Mrs. Young that, based on her Pelvic Ultrasound and laboratory results, that she will never be able to conceive or carry a child. She had massive fibroids, which in his words made it impossible for her to conceive.

The couple were devastated but rather than pin their hopes on man, they looked up to God. She joined the choir at the Assembly, strengthened her Kingdom focus, while Mr. Young became a dedicated member of the Men's ministry and served as an aide of the pastor.

After years of prayers, praise and passionate service to the saints and God, Mrs. Young conceived and had a baby girl at the age of thirty-eight! Even though it looked unlikely, if not impossible medically, her impossible-to-conceive anatomy, became the repository of a new-born baby boy because *"...with God all things are possible..."* (Matthew 19:26).

Life Lesson 43: Stop asking God for what man can do. Rather, ask Him for what only He can do!

"Let her sleep, for when she wakes she will move mountains"

– Facebook post on Kelly Langoria's comatose state
following her gun shot wound to the head

Chapter Forty-Four

Restoration, Revival
and Renewal!

"Behold, I will do a new thing; now it shall spring forth; shall ye not know it? I will even make a way in the wilderness, and rivers in the desert" (Isaiah 43:19).

K elly Kiper Langoria is the wife of the student, youth and music pastor at Life Church, Winnsboro, Louisiana. A December 2015 graduate of speech pathology from University of Louisiana Monroe (ULM), Louisiana, she is currently enrolled in a Masters of Speech pathology program at the same university.

On July 15th, 2016, she stopped at a convenience store on her way to work. While in the store, she was abducted, shot in the head and left for dead in a graveyard. She was found unresponsive by bystanders and airlifted to University of Mississippi Medical Center (UMMC) in Jackson, Mississippi. Unconscious and intubated, while on a ventilator, her prognosis was grim and chances of survival slim to none.

The reason for this grim prognosis was the bullet that remained in her head. It was in a difficult-to-remove position, and the neurosurgeons declined surgical intervention due to the risk involved. Since the consequences of taking the bullet out were too great a risk on Kelly's life, the neurosurgical team at UMMC decided to only stabilize and observe her.

The comeback kid

Kelly had lost her dad in November 2015, just after her marriage in June 2015. A devout Christian, she was known as a fighter for the faith and one who stood strong no matter how long for what she believed. Meanwhile, a *"Pray for Kelly"* movement started, and through social media, millions of people all around the world prayed for Kelly.

Nine days after her admission to UMMC, Kelly was sufficiently stable to come off the mechanical ventilator. She had control of her airway, moved the right side of her body sufficiently to throw a ball about seven feet and started speaking comprehensible words to her mother and husband. She commenced physical and speech therapy, and initially ambulated with assistance.

By December 2016, however, Kelly was speaking and walking without assistance. To the neurosurgical team attending to her, her recovery was nothing short of miraculous. While hospitalized, thousands all around the world were praying for Kelly, and God answered their prayer.

Today, Kelly is planning a return to ULM to complete her Masters degree in speech pathology. Even though she still has a long road ahead to full restoration of her speech and co-ordination of extremities, she has so far confounded science and delivered to a community of believers new-found faith in God!

Life lesson 44: God is too big to be estimated and too great to escape from!

What some call opposition,
God calls opportunity!

Chapter Forty-five

From Malignant to Miracle

"He (Jesus) cast out the spirits with his word, and healed all that were sick: That it might be fulfilled which was spoken by Esaias the prophet, saying, Himself took our infirmities, and bare our sicknesses" (Matthew 8:16-17).

D r. Frank is a medical doctor who went to medical school in Nigeria. He arrived in America at the turn of the millennium in pursuit of the American dream. Unfortunately, all he seemed to encounter were repeated nightmares. Rather than beg, however, Frank went about giving tennis lessons and playing the keyboard for several local churches to supplement his income.

In 2015, he was his usual ebullient self when he noticed blood in his stool. He followed up with his physician who referred him to a gastroenterologist for further work-up. He was in his early forties, and had no history of cancer in the family. He was, however, concerned with the altered bowel movements and profuse bleeding noticed on defecation.

After the colonoscopy, Frank was shocked to be told he had stage IV Colon cancer and was unlikely to live more than one year. He had never smoked cigarettes or drank alcohol, and yet was seemingly riddled with metastatic colon cancer.

Turning opposition into opportunity

Frank was devastated. He called his immediate family and friends who within a few weeks raised a sum of over $20,000.00 for him. He underwent surgical excision of the colon and began a six-month barrage of chemo and radiation therapy.

Frank, however, maintained an unaltered work schedule because of his financial situation. Even though his faith was challenged on several occasions, he remained resolute in thanksgiving to God and faith in Christ's atoning work on the cross of Calvary.

Six months later, Frank is cancer free and starting a new lease of life as an entrepreneur. His oncologists have termed his recovery a miracle and Frank's quick turnaround from cancer has stimulated positive interest from his classmates on supernatural healing.

What the devil meant for evil has rebounded for the cause of preaching the gospel for good! It is a signature response from the God of all the universe who said, in Hebrews 13:5-6, *"I will never leave thee, nor forsake thee. So that we may boldly say, The Lord is my helper, and I will not fear what man shall do unto me."*

Life Lesson 45: Those who reign in life go through the ridiculous with radical rejoicing and righteousness!

Faith is a mystery that gives you mastery over life's circumstances!

- Bishop David Oyedepo
(Presiding Bishop, Living Faith Church Lagos, Nigeria)

Chapter Forty-six

From Zero to Hero (Heart)

"My heart is fixed, O God, my heart is fixed: I will sing and give praise" (Psalm 57:7).

Allan and Jessica Green are an amiable couple who are an integral part of the Assembly, West Monroe, Louisiana along with their two lovely sons. Allan Green worked in the oil industry as an exploration operative, and in 2013 while working offshore he suddenly felt extremely short of breadth. He was in his mid-thirties at the time and had never felt so weak in his life.

He was whisked off by air ambulance to Oschner Medical Center, New Orleans, Louisiana where he was told by the in-house cardiologist that he had a near zero pumping heart. His ejection fraction was so abysmally low that the only solution in the long term was a heart transplant.

Immediately, prayers went up for Allan at the Assembly, West Monroe, Louisiana. Allan was added to an already burgeoning heart-transplant list, and sent home after a few weeks with a very grim prognosis. On his sick bed, however, Jessica and Allan prayed earnestly and asked God to fix Allan's heart.

The experiment, experience and engineering feat

Allan slowly became better and was eventually discharged from the hospital with approval for light duty. After six months of sick leave, his office assigned him to desk job responsibilities. Consequently, the family re-located to Houston, Texas where Allan's official responsibilities would take him.

Unfortunately, they moved into a house that had mold: and within three months Allan's health had steeply declined with experts in the field literally giving him up for dead at some of the most prominent hospitals in Houston, Texas. Rather than give up, however, Allan and Jessica persisted in prayer. They were persuaded God would come through for them.

After months of cardiac therapy with an external heart pump, Allan recovered and improved steadily in health. His memory that was sketchy throughout his near-fainting spells, was restored and he was able to ambulate and function with the assistance of the heart pump. At some of the most critical junctures of his life, only prayer sustained Allan.

In July 2016, after weeks of Allan's intubation secondary to the low output from the heart, Jessica returned to Monroe, Louisiana from Houston, Texas to see her children unsure of whether she would ever see Allan alive again. By the time she returned, however, Allan was awake and asking for his home-cooked meal. He had self-extubated the night before and was doing better without the ventilator.

Life Lesson 46: No prayer means no power; much prayer means much power!

I don't believe that God gave Austin autism; but I do know without a doubt that He did give us Austin.

- Joni Parsley
(wife of Rod Parsley, and mother of Austin Parsley).

Chapter Forty-seven

Austin Parsley: From Asperger's to Astounding!

"Trust in the LORD with all thine heart; and lean not unto thine own understanding. In all thy ways acknowledge him, and he shall direct thy paths. Be not wise in thine own eyes: fear the LORD, and depart from evil. It shall be health to thy navel, and marrow to thy bones" (Proverbs 3:5-8).

Austin Chandler Parsley was born July 11, 1991, to Pastor Joni and Rod Parsley. His birth was uneventful, but at two years of age his parents noted an unusually poor interaction with family and peers. He was easily distracted, increasingly irritable and filled with angst at the slightest provocation.

Austin's parents took him to a local pediatrician who did a psychoanalytic study on him. The test demonstrated a highly functioning Autistic Spectrum Disorder (ASD) called Asperger's Disorder, in Austin. This condition is part of the Pervasive Developmental Disorder (PDD) and has, according to medical expertise, no cure, with little hope for diagnosed individuals to ever accomplish anything concrete in life.

Pastors Rod and Joni Parsley were shocked. Their dream family had just been dealt a rude awakening. According to Joni, they had to transition from asking, *"Why did this happen to me?"* to *"I can't believe we were trusted by God to do this."*

From Nothing to Something

Rod and Joni Parsley stoutly rejected this medical prophesy of evil over their son! They refused to be deterred in their ministry but took it as a challenge for God to perform His word in their sons' life. They never ceased to believe God for their son, and continued to speak God's word – not medical terminology – over their son.

Austin proceeded to Harvest Preparatory elementary school and against all medical odds, he graduated and went to high school. In June 2010, he graduated with a 4.0 GPA from high school, spoke as the high school valedictorian and proceeded to Valor Christian college to do a Bachelor's degree in English and Linguistics.

Even though the pundits had expected Austin to recoil into his shell as he got older, he has grown bolder and is improving his public communication skills. They thought he would, at best, go to a vocational institute where he would work with appliances; but today Austin is a seasoned professional working amidst other professionals in pursuit of ministry.

Life Lesson 47: Loose lips sink ships; so, watch what you say!

It is not protocol, but altar call, God is interested in!

- Evangelist Reinhard Boonke
(International Evangelist and Founder Christ For All Nations)

Chapter Forty-eight

Jean Neil: Healed from the Heels to the Head

"Now unto him that is able to do exceeding abundantly above all that we ask or think, according to the power that worketh in us" (Ephesians 3:20).

Jean Neil suffered from lower back pain all through her teenage years. She went to a girls' home in Rugby England, where she was continually whipped and caned for living a mischievous life. She continued to suffer excruciating pain and underwent several surgeries to try to correct the defect, but it only grew worse.

After a long life of rebellion, she surrendered her life to Jesus Christ and became a Christian. Her husband, though not a believer, endured the ordeal of taking her back and forth to church in a wheel chair especially as she would constantly scream during the service when wracked with pain.

There was, however, no turning back for Jean. She continued to serve the Lord as a youth minister in her church. One day a three-year-old boy in the church, prayed for her asking God to heal her. That same night, in 1988, she had a dream in which a visiting foreign minister preached at a convention center, and in the dream she was immediately healed.

Taking back what the devil stole

Her faith was triggered by the dream. It gave her hope for a miracle again. In the summer of 1988, she attended a youth convention in which Reinhard Bonnke was the guest minister. She recognized his voice as that of the foreign evangelist who prayed for her in her dream.

While Jean sat in her wheel chair at the front of the auditorium, the Spirit of God told Reinhard Bonnke *"That woman in that wheel chair will be healed today."* After preaching to an overflow crowd of twelve thousand, of which fifteen hundred came to the altar to be saved, Reinhard went toward the sick and prayed for them.

The first person he prayed for in a wheel chair rebuffed him and so was not healed. At that moment, he remembered that God told him to go to the woman in the left side of the auditorium. He ran across the front of the auditorium and told Jean, *"You are going to be healed today."*

She replied, *"I know, I know, I know."* Apparently, just like in her dream, Bonnke had prayed for someone else before her who also was not healed due to unbelief! As soon as the Evangelist laid his hands on her, Jean slumped and fell forward under the power of God. She later described what she said were like surgical incisions going throughout her body. She got up at that juncture, and started to leap, jump and run all around the Birmingham Convention Center to the amazement of the capacity auditorium.

Her life never remained the same after that. When she woke up the next morning, she asked her still-doubting husband, *"Was it a dream?"* He replied, *"It was not a dream. It really happened. I was there."* She got out of bed, made breakfast, went shopping and ran up and down the stairs to her daughter's room in celebration of God's awesome works. Up till the writing of this book, Jean has continued to serve as a youth minister in her local congregation in Rugby, England and remains fully restored to health.

Life Lesson 48: If you must fall, fall forward in faith and not backward in doubt!

Part IV

Marriage Miracle

The key to the undeniable is seeing, hearing and speaking from the undetectable presence of God!

Chapter Forty-nine

Mr. D and His Miracle Recovery

"Men do not despise a thief, if he steal to satisfy his soul when he is hungry; But if he be found, he shall restore sevenfold; he shall give all the substance of his house" (Proverbs 6:30-31).

M
r. D is the eldest son of his parents, and in 2008 he lived in Southern Louisiana far away from home and the Christian ideals he had been brought up to imbibe. He and his wife had four lovely children but their marriage was continually ravaged by the debilitating effects of alcohol, cocaine and heroine.

In the midst of this tumultuous adventure, his father was burdened for his son and his family. On a Wednesday night prayer service, sometime in late 2008, Mr. D's father reached out to a pastor and asked him to agree with him for the salvation of his sons who were living a wayward life in south Louisiana.

Rather than pray, the pastor began to prophesy to the boys. He decreed them to return home and to believe the faith of their fathers. Within twenty-four hours, they younger son called his father and asked to return home. Seven days later, Mr. D called asking for his father's help. Rather than berate him for his drug habit that had truncated his destiny, his father welcomed him home.

The younger son returned to West Monroe, Louisiana, and went through drug and alcohol rehab and in 2013 took the leadership reins of the men's group at the local Church the family attended. Mr. D also returned home in 2008, underwent Christian alcohol and drug rehabilitation and today co-ordinates a recovery ministry for hundreds of former drug addicts in the West Monroe, Louisiana area.

Total Restoration

Since that prayer decree in 2008, the two sons have been drug free! The younger son is happily married with a stellar wife and two children. Mr. D, however, had a wife who did not want to change her drug habits. Unable to adjust to the demands of the new faith Mr. D was espousing, she left him and went back to Southern Louisiana.

Mr. D meanwhile was living a life of devotion to God when he met a young girl named Ms. J, who had also gone through multiple failed drug rehabilitation programs but had now surrendered her life to Christ. She was working as a para-legal, and had been drug-free for more than six months when she and Mr. D met.

After a period of dating, they married. Mr. D already had four children from his earlier marriage; but five years after he married Ms. J, they still had no children of their own. They went to their physician, and after investigations and laboratory tests, he told them, "*Ms. J can never have a baby.*"

The physician went on to advise the family to try Assisted Reproductive Techniques (ART) instead. As they were about to commence ART, via insemination and invitro fertilization (IVF) techniques, Ms. J discovered she was pregnant. Against all odds of medical science, God had planted a baby in a womb the medical professionals had labeled barren.

God had broken the yokes of barrenness and bondage to drugs and set the family in His fullness. Today, Mr. D and Ms. J are the proud parents of a lovely baby boy, lead ministers at a drug recovery program overseeing hundreds of ex-drug addicts and ecstatically publishing God's word with vigor and fervency.

Life Lesson 49: When the unstoppable meets the immoveable, the so-called immoveable must move!

Stay away from God's gold,
the girls, and His glory!

- Oral Roberts Mother's advise to her son as he entered ministry.

Chapter Fifty

From Rebel to righteous

"Forasmuch then as the children are partakers of flesh and blood, he also himself likewise took part of the same; that through death he might destroy him that had the power of death, that is, the devil; And deliver them who through fear of death were all their lifetime subject to bondage" (Hebrews 2:14-15).

M s. S had grown up as a church kid. Her parents were ardent members of a local church in the area and Ms. S was actively involved in the kids' Bible quiz team and fund-raising squad.

In her teenage years, Ms. S rebelled and began living a wayward life. She got involved in drugs and alcohol and soon began living a life of debauchery filled with perversion. She developed affinity for people of the same-sex and moved in with a same sex live-in-lover.

Her parents and siblings were appalled and appealed to her sense of conscience and responsibility, but to no avail. Her brother requested on one Sunday morning that the saints in the church pray for his sister's salvation. As they prayed, a turnaround miraculously began to occur!

The Rebel Returns

Some months after prayers went up for Ms. S's salvation, her brother stood on the pulpit to testify how God had delivered her from a lifestyle of lesbianism and lewdness. One day, while living a wayward lifestyle, she went to watch a movie called *"The Passion of the Christ"* by Mel Gibson.

She was awestruck by the graphic details of Jesus death and his expressive love for mankind. Without a preacher to lead her in the sinner's prayer, Ms. S knelt down in that cinema theatre and rededicated her life to following Jesus Christ.

She returned home, abandoned her wayward life and alternative lifestyle, and began attending Church regularly. Today, Ms. S is a grandmother, passionate about Jesus and epitomizes what extent the love of God can go to save a world knee-deep in poor choices.

Life Lesson 50: Those who give up their will for His will become willing in whatever is His will.

Laughter is the only Medicine
without any side-effects!

Chapter Fifty-one

Mrs. R: Fruitful mother battling a Frustrating life!

"Jesus answered and said unto her, Whosoever drinketh of this water shall thirst again: But whosoever drinketh of the water that I shall give him shall never thirst; but the water that I shall give him shall be in him a well of water springing up into everlasting life" (John 4:13-14).

Mrs. R is a thirty-one-year old dedicated wife and mother of two children. She and her husband have been married for more than ten years, and they relocated to West Monroe, Louisiana, from Florida for new job prospects.

Mrs. R had suffered a miscarriage in her second pregnancy that snowballed her into a whirlwind of depression. The miscarriage almost took her life because of excessive bleeding, and the attendant relocation to Louisiana compounded the issue by exhausting her physically and emotionally.

Her post-partum depression almost suffocated her spiritually. She was hearing strange voices and spent hours crying all day at home. Her husband took her to a psychiatrist, who placed her on antipsychotics and antidepressants. While navigating the new territory, she found the Assembly, West Monroe, Louisiana and she and her family quickly plugged into the church's activities.

Meanwhile her husband secured a job at a major institution

in Monroe, Louisiana. She enrolled as a Bible school student at the School of Urban Missions (SUM), West Monroe, Louisiana. Soon, she was pregnant again. The family were ecstatic but no one was more excited than Mrs. R. Things were, however, soon going to change in a staccato fashion for Mrs. R and her family.

Fighting against all odds from all fronts!

The domino started with the sudden death of Mrs. R's father in Florida while she was still two months pregnant. He had not been ill, but he fell down suddenly from a heart attack and died. Mrs. R had to go home for the funeral, leaving the children with her husband.

While trying to make sense of the sudden demise of her father and the inconsolable state of her mother, Mrs. R noticed she was bleeding incessantly from her pelvis area. She was about ten weeks pregnant at that stage. When she called her husband to seek his advice on what to do, he proffered immediate medical intervention. Because her insurance was only covered in Louisiana, however, he decided to bring her home to see her local physicians immediately.

The obstetricians evaluated her and decided to perform a dilatation and curettage on the twelve-week-old fetus because it was not viable. The termination of pregnancy procedure was uneventful, and afterwards Mrs. R went into severe major depressive disorder. She refused to go outside the home, was moribund having withdrawn from her Bible school course and would go three days at a stretch without sleeping.

Her husband, knowing these changes, informed her clinician of his wife's rapidly declining health. After a couple of changes to her medications, and many prayers, Mrs. R's mood improved markedly. Today, Mrs. R is back in Bible school, and acting as a loving mother of two children, doting wife and daughter to her husband and mother respectively.

Life Lesson 51: You may lose your goods, but never lose your joy, because if you keep that joy you will regain any goods!

There is nothing God has created that He cannot correct!

Chapter Fifty-two

Breakthrough in Belzoni

"...therefore take heed to your spirit, and let none deal treacherously against the wife of his youth. For the Lord, the God of Israel, saith that he hateth putting away: for one covereth violence with his garment, saith the Lord of hosts: therefore take heed to your spirit, that ye deal not treacherously" (Malachi 2:15-16).

M
r. and Mrs. R, a septuagenarian couple, have been married for more than fifty years. They invited my wife and I to their home in Mississippi sometime in 2014. While sharing a time of intimate fellowship, Mrs. R poured out her heart about her five decades-long relationship with her husband.

To our amazement, Mrs. R announced to us that she was filing for a divorce. She declared that her husband had not been supportive of her ministry and had continued to go to his home Church while she served as pastor of a charismatic church in Belzoni. She also felt he had not been a team player in the business and was ostracizing her from her staff and children.

This supposedly perfect couple who had built up their home-health business to include eighteen offices across three states, and had two wonderful children and several grandchildren, wanted to separate after fifty years of marriage. My wife and I took it as a challenge for God. We asked Him in prayer to heal their hurts, soothe their sorrows and mend their marriage.

Power Pass Power

My wife was particularly aghast! She kept reiterating her utter amazement at the R's marital condition, but I kept reminding her that God is a great restorer. On our knees and at the monthly Holy Ghost Night organized by our ministry – Faith and Power ministries – we lifted them up in prayers.

As a principle, my wife and I decided to speak life over the R's marriage. Instead of negative comments about them, we prophesied healing and restoration to their marriage. In our conversations, we spoke positive and affirming words toward them - not demeaning or hurtful words.

About a year later, in 2015, Mrs. R invited my wife and me to a gala night organized by her home-health company. She and her husband, oblivious of all other persons, took to the dance floor dancing lovingly and looking into each other's eyes. My wife and I were ecstatic! Only God could have healed a marriage so set on destruction.

Life Lesson 52: Death and life are in the power of the tongue; give good and you get good. Give garbage, and you get garbage!

*You don't need a makeover
when God makes you over!*

Chapter Fifty-three

Ms. T: Healed from the hurt!

"And when he (Jesus) had opened the book, he found the place where it was written, the Spirit of the Lord is upon me, because he hath anointed me to preach the gospel to the poor; he hath sent me to heal the brokenhearted, to preach deliverance to the captives, and recovering of sight to the blind, to set at liberty them that are bruised" (Luke 4:17-18).

Ms. T is the last and second child of her parents. Born in Northern Louisiana, the family relocated to Rayville, Louisiana, in her teen years and began attending a local Pentecostal church where she plugged into the kids' church activities.

As a result of a church dispute between her parents and the pastor, who they accused of swindling the church of thousands of dollars, Ms. T got estranged from Church. She stopped any church attendance in her late-teens and quickly nosedived into a life of sexual immorality and irresponsible behavior.

This *Rayville roller coaster* culminated in indelible scars that marred Ms. T for the rest of her life. She suffered emotional trauma at the hands of her parents, and was repeatedly molested sexually by a relative from seven years of age. This snowballed into depression and a life of promiscuity for Ms. T in her teenage and young adult years.

Persecuted for pedophilia; Pulled out for precious living!

After graduating from high school, Ms. T went on to college and studied nursing. Far away from home, Terry's sultry living only worsened. The mother of a sixteen-year-old boy, with whom she had had casual sex, reported her to the district attorney.

For the first time in a long time, Ms. T was afraid for her future. If convicted, she could face a life-long court-enforced barrier from handling children and possibly a life sentence in jail. In her moment of despair, she made a fresh commitment to Jesus Christ and asked Him to be the Lord and Savior of her life.

She asked God to fight for her, as she had no ability to fight this battle by herself. Her parents were incensed and refused to support her in anyway. She confessed to sleeping with an under-age minor, and was genuinely remorseful for her crime.

Miraculously, the district attorney dismissed the charges and wiped the case off the books forever. His doing so left a taste of God's mercy in Ms. T's heart that she has never forgotten. She turned her life around for God, enrolled in Bible College, and began ministering in the junior high ministry of the church.

Although she worked a fulltime job while in Bible school, she still graduated in July 2016 with stellar grades. In spite of her parents' lack of support towards her Bible school degree, Ms. T persevered. Today, she is a licensed minister with the Assemblies of God of USA and pursuing a ministry role in the children's ministry.

Furthermore, Ms. T has met and married the love of her life. He is a sold-out believer and she considers herself blessed to attract such a man of virtue in spite of her sordid past. Together, they hope to minister to the lost and the hurting especially in children's ministries all around the world.

Life Lesson 53: God is never late; He is always early or right on time!

What God has joined together,
don't let people mess it up!

– Apostle Ron Carpenter
(Snr. Pastor Redemption World Outreach
Center, Greenville, South Carolina)

Chapter Fifty-four

Ron Carpenter: Puppy love, Priestly loyalty, and Parental love

"He that hath an ear, let him hear what the Spirit saith unto the churches;
To him that overcometh will I give to eat of the hidden manna, and will
give him a white stone, and in the stone a new name written, which
no man knoweth saving he that receiveth it" (Revelation 2:17).

R on Carpenter is the senior pastor of Redemption World Outreach Ministries, Greenville, South Carolina with more than 30,000 members. The ministry has over twenty satellite churches, in the South Carolina and North Carolina area, and has seen rapid multiplication of ministries since its inception in 1991.

He is a third-generation preacher who went into ministry at the age of twenty-two. He has pursued God with a passion, and as a result has seen his ministry increase astronomically. His ministry is characterized by a fresh word and dynamic preaching that has turned millions around the world into champions in their fight for destiny.

He serves not only as shepherd of the sheep in his church but also as pastor and mentor to other pastors all over the world. He has crisscrossed the nations of the world preaching the gospel, published several books and is currently on world-wide television via Spanish and English language stations.

He has a passion for breaking down the walls of racism, sexism and class stratifications in the church. His Redemption World Outreach Church congregation, which is affiliated with the International Pentecostal Holiness Church, spans ten campuses and the home campus is home to about 19,000 members.

From Hope to Horrendous to Happy

Hope and Ron were married in 1991. After twenty-two years of marriage and three children, Pastor Ron Carpenter decided to break up with his wife, Hope, because of recurrent episodes of moral indiscretion and infidelity on her part. The world was shocked but no more so than the people of Greenville, South Carolina, who looked up to them as the ideal couple.

To the world, she was the ideal pastor's wife and worship leader. Ron had a different opinion, however. Even while they were undergoing counseling for an earlier indiscretion, Hope had yet another affair with an unnamed individual. He claimed Hope had a psychological problem relating to sexual affairs, and had therefore decided to end the union and place her in rehab until she was healed.

He categorically told the Church that he had no intention of reconciling with Hope and that their marriage was over. As he was about to file papers for the divorce, however, God arrested him and told him to call Hope back home. God told him, from Mark 10:1-11, that divorce was only for hardened hearts and, "... (as) *the wife of his youth,... the* LORD, *the God of Israel, saith that he hateth putting away*" (Malachi 2:15) of Hope.

In obedience, Apostle Ron called Hope and asked her to come back home. He announced to the church that he was taking his wife back and was determined to make his marriage work. They underwent a year of marriage counseling, and have seen restoration of the puppy love they once had for each other.

Their marriage is currently stronger than ever. The relationship served as a catalyst to heal racial and marital barriers in his local church and brought overflow to his life and ministry. Today, Ron testifies of a marriage with Hope that is like heaven on earth through God's miraculous intervention.

Life lesson 54: The road less travelled is the road most blessed!

Be the One percent the other Ninety Nine percent, who don't read the Bible, read and know about Christ Jesus!

Chapter Fifty-five

Breaking the spirit of rejection

"What do ye imagine against the Lord? He will make an utter end: affliction shall not rise up the second time" (Nahum 1:9).

Onyinye was in her second year of accountancy at the University of Nigeria, Enugu Campus (UNEC) in 2004. She had been inundated by a multitude of afflictions in her first year and, as she came to the annual anointing service of the Christian Union UNEC, she silently prayed to God for a quick turnaround in her fortunes.

She had jettisoned her nominal Christian status in the Roman Catholic Church and, as a result, her family had abandoned her and left her ostracized from friends and relatives with a severe loss in financial support the result. She had just barely scraped through her first year coursework, and had confided to her classmates in the campus fellowship that she may have to drop out if the mounting financial pressure upon her did not abate.

As the anointing service progressed, Onyinye was suddenly called out by name. The Preacher, Evangelist Emmah Isong, in the middle of his sermon suddenly declared that *"there is a girl called Onyinye here who has a mask upon her face that has plagued her with the spirit of rejection. He then warned *"refusal to get rid of that spirit and tear that spiritual mask off could be deleterious to her life as it spoke of grave danger in the future."*

The Power from on High!

Through the packed audience of more than two hundred, Onyinye slowly walked out of her seat, in the full view of the congregation with tears rolling them her face. She was not sure whether to be ashamed or relieved that a solution to her crisis of confidence had come.

The man of God then told her that a mask had been put over her spiritual face and destiny and that was why she had been going through unusual antagonism recently. He explained that the aim of the spiritual antagonists were to deter suitors from approaching her but that, as he lays hands upon her and the power of the Holy Spirit comes upon her, she would be free.

Onyinye received the word and as the man of God laid hands upon her, she screamed and fell under the power of God. Two years later, Onyinye finished her accounting degree in flying colors and maintained a fervent relationship with Christ throughout. She is currently an upwardly mobile and hugely successful accountant in Nigeria. Soon after graduation, she got married to her husband and together they have four children. Her destiny was drastically altered that day at the 1998 CU UNEC anointing service.

Life Lesson 55: What some call opposition, God calls opportunity!

There are only two kinds of people; Bitter and battered or blessed and better!

Chapter Fifty-six

From Miscarriage to miracle marriage

"...did not He make one? Yet had he the residue of the spirit. And wherefore one? That He might seek a godly seed. Therefore take heed to your spirit, and let none deal treacherously against the wife of his youth" (Malachi 2:15).

J ustin was unmarried, of Haitian heritage and had moved from New York to Monroe, Louisiana to study. After graduation, he went into entrepreneurship and opened a chain of taxi-cabs in the city. Leah, on the other hand, was an African American single parent who worked at a bank and after one failed relationship with her son's father was not willing to get hurt again.

After being introduced at a singles-event in Monroe, Leah and Justin decided to start attending the Assembly, West Monroe and they got actively involved in the Singles ministry. As new members of our local church, they attended the church's Valentine's Banquet in 2014 during which my wife and I sat next to them and fast acquainted ourselves with each other and so became good friends.

On a fateful Sunday, however, the stakes in their relationship were upped a lot! Pastor Shane Warren, the senior pastor, dropped a dare to anyone in the church that day. He said, *"If you are living together and are not married and want to get married, I will pay for your wedding if you cannot afford it!"*

Justin and Leah were living together at the time. Even though they were planning a wedding later in the year, they decided to take Pastor Shane up on his offer. They were married the following month, and within a few months Leah became pregnant. The newly-wedded couple were ecstatic, and enthusiastically sought ante-natal treatment.

Troubled, tested but triumphant!

Leah arrived at the doctor's office pensive and not sure what to expect. She had been bleeding for four days, and instead of going to the Emergency room she strolled into the doctor's office. Her last pregnancy had been complicated with high blood pressure and after doing a series of blood tests and ultrasounds, her worst fears were confirmed.

Leah and Justin's baby had died in utero. She had had an incomplete abortion and the baby in her womb was no more viable. They were shattered but undeterred in their love for each another. After evacuating the dead fetus, Leah was advised to give herself a few months to recuperate emotionally and physically before trying to conceive again.

Twenty-four months later, however, Leah was pregnant again. This time the pregnancy was uneventful, and she gave birth to a beautiful baby girl. Justin is expanding his cab business to adjoining cities, while Leah works as an administrator at a local business. They are both fulfilling their destiny, one child at a time.

Life Lesson 56: Death and Life are in the power of your tongue. Speak life and live!

Winners never quit and
quitters never win!

Chapter Fifty-seven

Miscarraige and Ministry

"And ye shall serve the LORD *your God, and he shall bless thy bread, and thy water; and I will take sickness away from the midst of thee. There shall nothing cast their young, nor be barren, in thy land: the number of thy days I will fulfill"* (Exodus 23:25-26).

D octors' Erinma and Chima Nnorom are some of the most delightful personalities a person can ever meet. Extremely warm and hospitable, they have been ardent supporters of the faith and Power Ministries my wife and I established in Louisiana on arrival in 2012.

As fellow Nigerians in the Bayou State, they helped us quickly settle into life in Louisiana and were, along with their adorable children, a constant source of well-being and homegrown support in our ministry adventures.

Chima, who is an ordained minister in his own right, would gladly drive up to Monroe, Louisiana from New Iberia, Louisiana, along with the rest of the family, to minister at our monthly Holy Ghost Night. Instead of taking finances from the ministry, he would instead give over and above his normal offering to the ministry.

God: The miracle-worker and miscarriage-wrecker

Unknown to my wife and me, Chima and Erinma had suffered two repetitious miscarriages. These unexpected miscarriages had occurred spontaneously and within the first trimester, to the shock of the medical personnel and family around them.

The Nnoroms, though heartbroken, refused to become hopeless. They continued to believe God's word notwithstanding their circumstances, and ramped up their service in God's vineyard. Chima became the head of the prayer ministry at his local congregation in New Iberia, Louisiana, and Erinma persisted in caring for her two young children.

They prayed for another baby and God answered. This time the baby lived till delivery, and both mother and child did well. They called their baby girl, *Chizara*, which means *God answers*. She is a testimony to God's answer to their prayers.

Life Lesson 57: To go backward is to remain barren for life!

You are a conduit of blessings,
not a container of baggage!

Chapter Fifty-eight

No return ticket

"And I will restore to you the years that the locust hath eaten, the cankerworm, and the caterpiller, and the palmerworm, my great army which I sent among you (Joel 2:25).

Mr. and Mrs. Hogan attended the Assembly, West Monroe, Louisiana and were ardent members of the *relentless* Sunday school group my wife and I attended. They were going through a tough time matrimonially, and sought counsel in their throes.

My wife and I asked them to reconcile, as the allegations of misdemeanor against the husband were unsubstantiated. For Mrs. Hogan, however, the die was cast and she insisted on an immediate divorce and nothing else. Other members of the church tried to intervene but to no avail.

She moved out of their home in West Monroe in Northern Louisiana and moved to her sister's residence in New Iberia, south Louisiana. The family, which consisted of six children and ten grandchildren, were distraught. Prayers were offered for the family by the church and close friends even though it looked like Mrs. Hogan's mind was made up.

The point of return!

The Hogans' had been married for over thirty-five years and were an exemplary couple to other believers in our local community till this marital fracas broke out. At the monthly Holy Ghost Night organized by the ministry I superintend, we prayed for a restoration of their union.

One day, while in New Iberia, Louisiana Mrs. Hogan heard God speaking to her asking her to return to her home. He told her to forgive all hurts from her past, and love her husband unconditionally. She was to return immediately and with unreserved apologies to the family and friends for her recent conduct.

On hearing God's instructions, Mrs. Hogan called the lawyers handling the divorce proceedings and asked them to cease forthwith. She moved back home to be with her husband in West Monroe, Louisiana, and today they are more in love with one another than ever before.

Life Lesson 58: If you want to go fast, go alone but if you want to go far go together!

No man can demean what Christ has esteemed!

-Archbishop Benson Idahosa (1939-1996)

Chapter Fifty-nine

From Frustration to Fruitful!

*"Rebuke not an elder, but in treat him as a father; and the
younger men as brethren; The elder women as mothers; the
younger as sisters, with all purity"* (1 Timothy 5:1-2).

Ms. K is a seventeen-year-old Caucasian female who lives
in the North-eastern part of Louisiana. She was abused
sexually as a child by her Father, who was also the youth
pastor of their church. As a result of her experience, she suffered
posttraumatic stress, severe anxiety and inhibited social skills.

Her father, meanwhile, was dismissed from the pastorate,
incarcerated and placed on a lifelong pedophilia watch list that limited
him from interacting with children without supervision. As a result
of the fallout of the incident in the community, Ms. K and her siblings
moved out of Southern Louisiana to northern Louisiana with their
mother.

The intention of the relocation was to enable the children grow up
without any form of recriminations from society. Ms. K, as the eldest
child, took the disappointment to heart, and it took a toll on her health.
She enrolled in home schooling, instead of public school, to avoid
social interactions with the public. This lack of social interactions
eventually snowballed into severe depression and anxiety for Ms. K.

Hemangioma, Healing and Hallelujah

Ms. K had once professed faith in Christ and considered herself a believer. After moving to North east Louisiana, she soon joined a local Church. As she began to interact with her peers in the Church, her faith grew and so did her love for the word of God. She refused to wallow in her past, but resolved to follow God into her future.

She maintained stellar grades in her school work and as high school graduation neared, she applied to several Christian colleges for admission. Even though she was rejected by several of them for physical frailty and psychological fluidity, Ms. K refused to be daunted. She believed God's word that she was His *"...treasure in earthen vessels, that the excellency of the power may be of God, and not of us"* (2 Timothy 4:7).

She was eventually accepted into one of the top Christian colleges in the nation after persisting with the application process. She wants to go as far as possible in her college education, and thereafter pursue her destiny in the ministry.

A massive hemangioma, measuring 25cm x 20cm, meanwhile developed on her abdomen. It did not amend to conservative measures, and surgical microabrasive surgery was recommended. Notwithstanding the stigma and sicknesses that have been tagged on her, Ms. K never fails to see herself as the epitome of beauty and femininity and does not feel inferior to her colleagues in any way.

Life Lesson 59: Change your thoughts, and you will change your life quickly!

When you are surrounded by celebration, you avert crises!

Chapter Sixty

Lost and found

*"Behold, I will send you Elijah the prophet before the coming of the
great and dreadful day of the Lord: And he shall turn the heart of the
fathers to the children, and the heart of the children to their fathers,
lest I come and smite the earth with a curse"* (Malachi 4:6).

Fifteen-year old Master T was at the supermarket with his mom,
when the unexpected and unforeseen happened. His mom
grabbed him forcibly from her side of the car and dragged
him on the floor. Passersby called the police. Within fifteen minutes,
Master T's mom was incarcerated and Master T was placed in foster
care.

His grandmother, who is an ardent member of her local church and
the faith and power ministries which I superintend, was devastated.
She asked that prayers be made for him at our July 2015, Holy Ghost
Night. She was concerned that his current foster home was inflicting
multiple infringements on his religious and moral freedom to worship.

Petition was made to heaven by the saints. Master T's grandmother,
meanwhile, applied to the courts for re-instatement as his legal
guardian. The judge listened to her argument and sent social workers
to evaluate his living conditions. Her daughter, who is Master T's
mother, was released from prison and opted to move into her own
house. This was the last threat to Master T's return, and now the

obstacle had been cleared, Master T's and his grandmother were free to reconnect.

Invalid or invaluable?

Master T's started attending a new junior high school and was repeatedly bullied and made fun of by his peers for his lanky appearance. To top it all, however, some of his middle school colleagues started spreading rumors that he had an alternative lifestyle since he did not befriend girls.

All these made Master T's grandmother even more desperate to get him out of his current living conditions. She felt that there were pedophiles or homophobic males with malevolent tendencies in the foster home he dwelt in and their presence affected her grandson negatively.

Eventually, after taking in opinions from the medical, educational, family and social spheres, the judge released Master T back to his mother. He was free to attend church, unlike when he was at his erstwhile foster home, and one of the first places he visited on being reunited with his Grandmother was our monthly Holy Ghost Night.

He testified about his decision, while separated from his family to follow Jesus unconditionally. After prayers and prophesies were made over him that night, Master T is standing strong as a stalwart of the gospel. His academics and social interaction skills have improved. Now, he is looked at as invaluable and not as an invalid!

Life Lesson 60: What men call rejects, God calls repairers of the breach!

The spirit of revelation is
the spirit of revival!

Chapter Sixty-one

Ms. K: A life spared and star spangled

"I will ordain a place for my people Israel, and will plant them, and they shall dwell in their place, and shall be moved no more; neither shall the children of wickedness waste them anymore, as at the beginning" (1 Chronicles 17:9).

A t the age of twelve, Ms. K's mother was left homeless by her drunken husband. After several fist fights and drunken orgies, involving Ms. K's mother, her stepfather was arrested by the police and incarcerated. This left Ms. K's mom as the sole breadwinner of the family and, because she had no source of income at the time, she left their apartment and moved into a battered women's shelter.

The plight of Ms. K's family came to the attention of a "Good Samaritan" named Ms. A. Though she was already the mother of two boys and a girl, she took Ms. K home one night after seeing her plight and five years later, Ms. K still lives with her and her husband as their fourth child.

The entire family, including Ms. A's parents and parents-in-law received Ms. K with open arms. Today that once-abandoned girl is the epitome of beauty and virtue. Ms. K's mother was so challenged by Ms. A's generosity that she surrendered her life to Jesus Christ and submitted herself to Teen Challenge for a one year drug rehabilitation program.

From homeless to heiress

Ms. K is in High school currently and actively preparing to go to college. She believes she escaped the scourge of drugs, which enveloped her family and led to multiple incarcerations including that of her mother and brothers, because she moved in with Ms. A.

Out of six members of her family, only Ms. K has not served a prison sentence. The rest have had multiple run-ins with the law, convicted for distribution and use of substances of abuse and are recurrent alcoholics. Ms. K, however, is the exception. She loves the lord with all her heart and is an ardent worshipper of God and his people. Even though her biological mother is hardly in her life, Ms. K knows she has an everlasting father who "....*will never leave or forsake her...*" (Matthew 28:20).

Her senior brother has spent more time in jail than he has being free since turning into an adult. The misadventure of her past has not relinquished Ms. K from aspiring for her dreams. She has a family that loves her, a senior brother called *Jesus Christ* that looks out for her on every turf and a heavenly father that would never abuse her but has promised to use her to "...*shew forth the praises of him who hath called you out of darkness into his marvelous light* " (1 Peter 2:9).

Life Lesson 61: What men call a mistake, God calls a miracle!

The life of immediately causes interruptions to satanic manipulations

Chapter Sixty-two

Rejoicing amidst their rejection

"Let thy fountain be blessed: and rejoice with the wife of thy youth. Let her be as the loving hind and pleasant roe; let her breasts satisfy thee at all times; and be thou ravished always with her love" (Proverbs 5:18-19).

Patricia is the third child and first daughter of her parents. Born in the Eastern part of Nigeria, she grew up with a keenly analytical mind that enabled her graduate with stellar grades from a University in Nigeria in biomedical science and physiotherapy.

She moved to the United States in pursuit of a medical graduate degree. While everyone else was excited at her imminent travel plans, a sullen aunty told her *"over my dead body will you ever get married."*

Patricia did not pay attention to her aunty's vituperations, but dismissed it as the grievances of a despondent woman. Twenty years later, however, the words of this aunty were proving true! While her contemporaries were getting married at the drop of a hat, Patricia had no suitors.

One Prayer Changes Everything

On a wet wintery weekend in Maryland, USA my wife and Patricia were in deep conversation when she beckoned me to come over. She had intimated my wife on the "curse" her aunty had spoken over her, and my wife wanted us to pray for her before we departed for Louisiana.

I prayed the law of attraction over her by calling upon God to cause *"...many to make suit unto her"* (Job 11:19) in Jesus name. Within three months, God had turned Patricia's rejection into rejoicing. A Nigerian lawyer, in Port-Harcourt, Nigeria, heard about her through a mutual acquaintance. Within two months of courtship they were engaged, and soon after married.

The aunty who had vowed to die rather than see Patricia get married was alive to see God turn her captivity. Even though she was in her early forties, at the time of her wedding, God proved that He alone is the architect of marriage and that no man can stop His plans.

Life Lesson 62: Don't let your enemy stop your rejoicing!

You can never be more like God until you do something for someone who can't repay you!

Chapter Sixty-three

From Prisoner to Pastor to Parent!

"Rid me, and deliver me from the hand of strange children, whose mouth speaketh vanity, and their right hand is a right hand of falsehood: That our sons may be as plants grown up in their youth; that our daughters may be as corner stones, polished after the similitude of a palace" (Psalm 144:11-12).

Ms. S is a beautiful thirty-one-year-old Caucasian female who was incarcerated in 2014 for drug usage and distribution. While in prison, however, she was apprehended for Christ by the Holy Spirit as a group of women (including my wife, Rita Momah) ministered to them.

The power of the gospel touched her at her lowest ebb; and as she held on to God's word to deliver her from modern-day idols, she placed her faith once again in the Lord Jesus Christ. With trust in God for a breakthrough, the judge suddenly gave her leave to attend a drug rehab program spear-headed by the Christian organization Teen Challenge.

At the Louisiana Teen Challenge hostel, she busied herself with studying the word of God and learning homemaker skills such as sewing and cooking. She already had two teenage children from past relationships, and had no intention of ever remarrying-until she met Mr. D.

He was a young itinerant preacher and technician who drove six hours to-and-from to preach and teach at the Teen Challenge camp in Dodson, Louisiana, every Friday. On one occasion, while Mr. D was preaching, God told Ms. S that the young preacher would one day be her husband. She shuddered at the thought, but soon after it was confirmed when Mr. D invited Ms. S to his home to meet his parents who were third-generation preachers with the Assemblies-of-God.

From condemnation to celebration

In May 2015, Mr. D and Ms. S married. Ms. S then moved in with Mr. D, alongside her two children, to be a wife and mother. At about the same time, the Lord led Mr. D to relinquish his position as a technician to go into full-time ministry. He took a position with a local church as the senior pastor and Ms. S became a Pastor's wife.

At this juncture, Ms. S was seen in a local clinic and after been diagnosed and treated for her presenting complaints, found out incidentally that she was six weeks pregnant. The couple were surprised but ecstatic, as this would be their first child as a couple. From a repeat jailbird to a newly-wed pastor's wife and mother-to-be, it all seemed so surreal to Ms. S.

Ms. S had suffered much condemnation for her sullied past, but God was celebrating her now with the promise of a family and a husband that cherished her. She is no more an outcast of society, nor an eyesore to the public, but a crown on her husband's head and the apple of God's eye.

Life Lesson 63: Affirmation makes for assimilation, but the anointing creates an awakening of destiny.

*If the demoniac of Gadarenes
ran and worshipped Jesus, then
there is no devil that can stop
a believer living for Jesus!*

Chapter Sixty-four

From satan to *summa cum-laude!*

"Neither is there salvation in any other: for there is none other name under heaven given among men, whereby we must be saved" (Acts 4:12).

Mr. and Mrs. E are dear friends of my wife and me. As one of the first families we met in Monroe, Louisiana, they have been an invaluable asset as friends, prison-ministry mentors and Church members. They have exemplified Christian passion and peerless commitment to us and several other families in the area by going beyond and above their call of duty.

When they asked my wife and me to pray for their son Mr. C we passionately sought the face of God for him. Mr. C, even though he had been brought up in church and had learned the scriptures as a child, had gone into drugs and sinful living. While working offshore, Mr. C had veered into the occult and, on his return home refused to go to church with his parents. Instead, he would spend nights partying with questionable characters.

The situation degenerated to the extent that Mr. E on one occasion called the law enforcement agencies to lock Mr. C up at a prison hospital for untoward and violent behavior. He had been behaving inappropriately and his father suspected he had been using Phencyclidine (PCP) and was on the verge of a mental breakdown.

In the face of satan

After been released from the hospital prison, Mr. C disappeared and his parents could not find him. They asked for emergency prayers, and at one our monthly Holy Ghost Night services, the saints in the house travailed for Mr. C until we felt God give us a breakthrough.

Within twenty-four hours of those prayers, Mr. C was found. He had stumbled into a Pentecostal Church, accepted Jesus as his Lord and savior and been filled with the Holy Ghost with the evidence of speaking in other tongues. The change was so dramatic and sudden it almost scared his parents.

The following Sunday, Mr. C was in Church with his parents albeit willingly. He became not just a committed-church-goer, who served alongside his dad as an usher, but also enrolled as a student of the School of Urban Missions (SUM) Bible college hosted by the church.

He spent three years in the college, and goes in the face of satan preaching the gospel at events such as *Mardi-Gras* and other inner city revivals. On one of those trips, he met a young lady who also happened to be a student of SUM, and in November 2016 they got married. He is on track for a summer 2017 *Summa-Cum Laude* grade point graduation and hopes to go into the ministry with his newly wed wife as soon as he graduates.

Life Lesson 64: Miracles don't take time, but they always require truth!

Abide in God so you may
abound in Him!

Chapter Sixty-five

Killer Turned Pillar

"For I will take you from among the heathen, and gather you out of all
countries, and will bring you into your own land. Then will I sprinkle clean
water upon you, and ye shall be clean: from all your filthiness, and from
all your idols, will I cleanse you. A new heart also will I give you, and a
new spirit will I put within you: and I will take away the stony heart out
of your flesh, and I will give you an heart of flesh" (Ezekiel 36:24-26).

Apostle T came to my office bemoaning the tragedy that had
befallen his family. His grandson in Dallas, Texas, had fatally
shot a young man at pointblank range and was being held by
the police for murder.

He had ministered at the Holy Ghost Night organized by Faith and
Power Ministries, which my wife and I oversee. I reassured him that
the saints would uplift his son in prayer. I told him God is a now-God
who can change even the most dire of circumstances.

He left encouraged, but he was still crestfallen. He believed that
bad friends had beclouded his grandson's judgment and that he had
failed as his grandfather to turn back the tide of evil that had now
swallowed up his grandson.

The Power of Prayer

The saints at our Holy Ghost Night meeting took the grandfather's
plea to our prayer altar. We poured out our hearts for the young man

and sent the Word of God to his cell calling forth restoration and deliverance in his life. We pulled down any strongholds and planted the seed of the Word of God in his heart, using Proverbs 22:6 as the basis for our prayers.

In less than a month, the story had changed. According to his grandfather, the grandson had become a Christian in prison and turned his life over to Christ. Even more glaring of the supernatural intervention in his life, this grandson conceded to enter a plea bargain with the Texas Department of Justice. He had earlier denied the charges, but with the plea-bargain he would see the death sentence he would have been given, reduced to a lighter sentence.

His grandfather and I were thrilled. This youthful killer had turned into a pillar in the Texas prison community. He was leading prayer meetings, starting revivals and preaching to fellow inmates. He was truly a new man, and exemplifies the gospel as the "...*power of God unto salvation to everyone that believeth*..." (Romans 1:16).

Life Lesson 65: Problems putrefy or purify depending on one's persuasions.

Part V

Ministers' Miracles

- Saved by the bell of the Holy Spirit
- Boy in the boot
- The miracle of medicine, a made-up mind and a master who heals
- Turnaround testimony
- Living in the supernatural
- Nigerian evangelist with three kids after years of barrenness
- John Kohlenberger: A meteorite with trailblazing revelation
- Heidi's husband's healing
- The 40th birthday surprise
- John Hagee: A modern-day Moses
- Chrissy Cymbala: A turnaround testimony
- The girl kidnapped at Winner's chapel
- Mariah Todd: Bred in fire and birthed by faith!
- The Apostle of always joy
- Shane Warren: From heart patient to healthy Pops
- From Bakavu to breakthrough
- Rod Parsley: From silent to silent no more
- Casey Treat: Healed from Hepatitis C
- Bishop Jones: From healer to healed
- Is anyone dead here?
- Lea Joyner: Pioneer preacher and martyred minister!
- Tyler Cook: Delivered from drugs!
- Pastor Foster: Healed by the blood of Jesus!

- Gary Bethley: From Zero to hero
- Carman: Back from the dead
- David Oyedepo: Healed from tuberculosis
- John Hagee's daughter: Healed of Leimyosarcoma of the lung
- Eddie Jackson: Ministry and medical miracle candidate
- Amy Givler's supernatural child birth
- Marilyn Hickey: God's signs and wonders woman
- Lester Sumrall and the strange story of Clarita Villaneva
- David Remedios: From the streets to the stars
- E.A Adeboye: Terrible to the enemy, terrific to the elect
- Oral Roberts: Healed miraculously from Tuberculosis
- Dr. Jesse Duplantis and God's surgery

Those who attain mastery
in life refused to tolerate
mediocre living.

Chapter Sixty-six

Saved by the bell of the Holy Spirit

"And though the Lord give you the bread of adversity, and the water of affliction, yet shall not thy teachers be removed into a corner any more, but thine eyes shall see thy teachers: And thine ears shall hear a word behind thee, saying, This is the way, walk ye in it, when ye turn to the right hand, and when ye turn to the left" (Isaiah 30:20-21).

Ms. L is an elegant African American female in the Monroe community. Her medical history includes a litany of medical conditions as a result of several emotional, psychological, social, physical and financial abuse at the hands of her family and ex-husbands. Notwithstanding her background and the odds stacked against her, Ms. L is determined to raise her three children in the fear of the Lord.

After temporary loss of her children, following custody battles with their fathers, Ms. L was restored to her children's lives. She watched as two of them proceeded into college and one sauntered seamlessly through high school. She made an effort to reconcile with her mother, who treacherously had gotten the children removed from her on charges of Ms. L being an unfit mother, and even started a ministry.

In addition to her spiritual and maternal responsibilities, Ms. L was also a para-legal. After losing her job at a prominent bank, she brushed up her skills and reapplied for a job in a legal firm. She was hired nearly immediately and moved into a secluded and supposedly safe neighborhood. Her world was, however, about to unravel in spite of her neatly sculptured and formatted plans for her life.

A Moment's whisper and a mother's wisdom

As Ms. L came out of her house one weekday morning, she saw a young African American male running toward her car. He asked her matter-of-factly for a ride, but as Ms. L looked into his steely cold gaze she knew something was not right.

She turned down his request for a ride and quickly retreated into her house and bolted the door. At that point, she noticed on local television that there was an ongoing manhunt and the man she had just seen was responsible for murdering a local cop in cold blood.

At this juncture, Ms. L quickly alerted the authorities. She pointed them in the direction he went and after a three hour man-hunt he was apprehended. He had snug into the attic of Ms. L's neighbors' house and may have escaped if she had not alerted them on his escape route. This twenty-one year old has been charged with theft, drug smuggling and murder of a police officer.

Finally, it dawned on Ms. L that God had just delivered her from the hands of a very dangerous criminal. For that she continues to give God glory and honor. When she was whiskers away from being kidnapped or killed by this murderer, she escaped because of the still small voice of the Holy Spirit that directed her.

Life Lesson 66: When you see the invisible, you can do the impossible!

*The Church fights, not for the
victory, but from a position
of victory in Christ!*

Chapter Sixty-seven

Boy in the Boot!

"For the eyes of the LORD run to and fro throughout the whole earth, to shew himself strong in the behalf of them whose heart is perfect toward him..." (2 Chronicles 16:9).

Ten-year old Willie Myrick was standing in his Atlanta front yard on March 31, 2014, when he saw some money on the ground. As he bent to pick it up, a man suddenly appeared from nowhere, and abducted him and put him in the trunk of his car. His abductor commanded him to keep silent and not say a single word.

Willie, however, started singing the famous song composed and performed by Hezekiah Walker titled *Every praise is to our God*. The words of the song resonated throughout the car, and after driving around the east side of Atlanta for three hours, the kidnapper was exasperated and demanded Willie get out of the car at the next junction and to tell no one about what just happened.

Willie did not relent but kept singing the song because, as he later testified, he knew God would invade his location if he praised him! This song he had learnt at Sunday school, had long been a favorite of Willie's and he chose to shout God's praise notwithstanding the gargantuan obstacles in his way.

Lost and Found

Meanwhile, Willie's parents' were aghast at his sudden disappearance. They notified the police and soon a missing person's request was made for him. They searched all the suburbs with no success. Then suddenly Willie's parents got a phone call from a passerby identifying Willie as being in his driveway.

Immediately after the call, the police picked up little Willie. Using Willie's memory, they were able to sketch a pictorial of the kidnapper. He was an African American male in his late twenties with no criminal record. Police considered Willie lucky to have escaped from his clutches.

The parents, however, believe that this was a miracle not just a lucky escape. They were ecstatic to be reconnected with their precious son. A $10,000.00 reward was placed for information towards the arrest of the kidnapper. Meanwhile, Willie has continued to travel around the United States testifying and declaring that *Every praise belongs to our God.*

Life Lesson 67: Whatever God does is forever!

Tomorrow is only as bright as the lens you look at them through!

Chapter Sixty-eight

The miracle of medicine, a made-up mind and a Master who heals

"Take heed in the plague of leprosy, that thou observe diligently, and do according to all that the priests the Levites shall teach you: as I commanded them, so ye shall observe to do. Remember what the Lord thy God did unto Miriam by the way, after that ye were come forth out of Egypt" (Deuteronomy 24:8-9).

B ishop Harry Jackson is a prominent African-American pastor in the Washington D.C. area. As the Convener of the Reconciled Church Conference, Chairman of the High Impact Leadership Coalition, Presiding Bishop of the International Communion of Evangelical Churches and Senior Pastor of Hope Christian center Beltsville, Maryland, Bishop Harry Jackson is a man of visibility and violent-taking faith.

In 2005, however, his faith was shaken to the core. His physicians told him that he had esophageal cancer that was already metastatic (stage three) and he had less than a ten percent chance of survival. As he was being prepared for surgery and radiation cum chemotherapy, he suffered a stroke that paralyzed half of his body. This Harvard-trained MBA professional, husband and father looked down at his life and saw it ebbing away.

In the quiet of his hospital room, while this calamity was going on, Bishop Jackson dedicated himself back to God and chose life instead of death. In spite of the gruesome procedures he had to undergo, including a seven-and-a-half hour surgical procedure to reposition his esophagus on his birthday, and feeding through a feeding tube for months, Bishop Jackson refused to be deterred.

Defeating doubt by destiny desires!

Bishop Harry testifies about how, thirteen years later, he is not only alive but thriving and cancer-free in his new book *You Were Born to Be More: Six Steps to Breaking Through to Your Destiny.* He tells how in the throes of self-pity and at the door of death, God Himself put something inside him resolving him to live.

Instead of disillusionment and despondency, Bishop Harry chose to live out his destiny according to the freedom that Christ has ordained for believers. He called his church, ministry friends and partners. Together, they ambushed the gates of hell and assailed the throne of God with petitions, supplications and travailing prayers for the life of Bishop Harry Jackson.

God answered by fire and gave Bishop Harry Jackson life when all the naysayers had stamped death at his door. Today, he is an avid social conservative commentator and a leading voice for an all-integrated church across race, tribe or creed especially as it concerns faith and God's people in the D.C. area.

His experience with cancer has taught Bishop Jackson to trust in the Lord at all times without compromise. Even though he developed arrhythmia as a fall-out of his therapy, and his wife followed soon afterwards with breast cancer, Bishop Jackson believes that the healing power of God has given him a renewed sense of mission in life. As a result, he pursues the fixing of societal and spiritual ills with an unrelenting passion.

Life Lesson 68: The power to see the impossible starts with seeing the invisible God at work in you!

"If God can remove a mountain, he can remove a cyst!"

- Pastor Brad Smith, Lead Pastor First Assembly of God
Monticello, Arkansas USA (Paraphrasing Mark 11:23-24)

Chapter Sixty-nine

Turnaround Testimony

"He sent his word, and healed them, and delivered them from their destructions" (Psalm 107:20).

Pastor Brad Smith is the Lead pastor of First Assembly of God Church, Monticello, Arkansas USA. In February 2015, while a pastor in Pineville, Louisiana, he felt abdominal cramps and went to a nearby urgent care center for treatment. Because of the severity of the pain, a Computerized Tomography (CT) scan was ordered and a left sided complex cyst within his kidney measuring 3 by 3cm was found.

He was given a grim diagnosis. The supervising urologist believed that the position of the cyst was an indicator of renal carcinoma and recommended they wait four months to see if the cyst grows or stabilizes. A month later, while standing on Mark 11:23-24, Pastor Brad Smith came out to be prayed for at the Louisiana Women's district convention hosted by his church.

The minister, Steve Mcknight, laid hands on his back and something shifted in Brad Smith that night. This occurred on March 20th, 2015 and when Brad returned to the urologist on Tuesday May 5th, 2015, a repeat CT scan was done. Three days later, the urologist called him and to his pleasant surprise told him *"the mass had disappeared."*

The trouble terminator!

The urologist said only a scar was noticeable on the CT Scan where the left renal mass was located. He said, *"it almost looked like somebody had already cut it out!"* Pastor Brad then told him it was nothing short of a miracle and the urologist added *"a strange one."*

Throughout Pastor Brad's strange ailment, he had been unequivocal in speaking faith and truth to his mountain. He told whoever cared to listen that if Jesus said speak to mountains and they be cast into the sea, He can surely remove a cyst if we speak His word! He continually declared himself healed and so walked victoriously over cancer.

Pastor Brad believes his miracle took place on the night he humbled himself and got prayed for at a women's convention by a travelling evangelist, even though he was the host minister. Till today, Pastor Brad Smith has a clean bill of health and has shared his testimony all around the world with God confirming it with signs and wonders following.

Life lesson 69: Those who trouble their troubles will never be troubled again!

*Not all of us can do great
things. But we can all do small
things with great love!*

- Mother Teresa (1910-1997)

Chapter Seventy

Living in the supernatural

"Can a woman forget her sucking child, that she should not have compassion on the son of her womb? yea, they may forget, yet will I not forget thee. Behold, I have graven thee upon the palms of my hands; thy walls are continually before me" (Isaiah 49:15-16).

Bill Wilson, is the senior pastor of Metro World child ministries headquartered in Brooklyn, New York, USA. He pioneered multiple means of reaching the youth in Brooklyn, New York and currently sees more than one hundred thousand children under the age of twelve bussed in on Sunday mornings to attend Sunday school.

All through life, however, Bill has been a bundle of supernatural testimonies. He was abandoned as a twelve-year old by his mother who left him on a street corner in Pinellas Park, Florida, USA for three days. A mechanic, Dave Rudenis, saw him and took him home. When no one would come up to claim little Bill Wilson, this mechanic and his wife decided to adopt him.

They sent him to a summer church camp where Bill committed his life to Christ. He went on to graduate from high school and afterwards headed to seminary. He attended Southeast Assembly of God University, Lakeland, Florida, and obtained a degree in Theology and ministry.

Leader, lover and lifter

Billy Wilson has gone on to inspire a generation of fatherless youth who so direly need a father in their lives. He resonates what God can do with a man or woman, even when they are rejected by their own biological family.

After graduating from Bible school, Bill returned to his home church near St. Petersburg, Florida and pioneered one of the first bus ministries in the USA. Together with his fellow ministers, they picked up thousands of children from the inner cities of St. Petersburg and taught them a Bible message containing music, toys and games.

He went on to replicate the successes achieved in Florida in Davenport, Iowa and finally Brooklyn, New York. He has become a veritable voice for the innercity child and is credited with raising millions of dollars for inner city children all around the world.

Life lesson 70: Yesterday is a tomb, while today is the womb for tomorrow's boom.

"Outside the will of God, there is nothing I want. Inside the will of God, there is nothing I fear"

- A.W Tozer (1897-1963).

Chapter Seventy-one

Nigerian evangelist with three kids after years of barrenness

"...it came to pass, when I prophesied, that Pelatiah the son of Benaiah died. Then fell I down upon my face, and cried with a loud voice, and said, Ah Lord GOD! wilt thou make a full end of the remnant of Israel?" (Ezekiel 11:13).

Evangelist Tinuke was married for fifteen years without having a child. The doctors had said nothing was wrong with her or her husband. In the ensuing circumstances, she and her husband separated several times. As the only son of his parents, and their only hope for future descendants, the predicament of not having a child compounded an already volatile situation and robbed their marriage of the needed peace and love it needed.

It was at this point that Evangelist Tinuke went to a Pentecostal Church in Nigeria. At the first deliverance service she attended, she prayed with everything in her. She poured out her heart overnight before God. She prayed prayers that night in a special way and even used clubs or anything she could lay her hands on to fight her enemies.

After she arrived home the next morning, her husband received a call from the village that his mother's sister was seriously ill and was near death. On her death bed, she had confessed to being responsible for Evangelist Tinuke's woes. She claimed Evangelist Tinuke did not pay attention to her, or greet her well on the day she wedded her nephew.

She had thus labeled Evangelist Tinuke as a proud person deserving of physical barrenness. Soon after her confession, this aunty to Tinuke's husband died.

Death by divine decree

Evangelist Tinuke was shocked at the rapid turn of events. She did not want the death of her husband's aunty but she attributed it, nonetheless, to her prayers the night before. She prayed for God to take away her problems and He did.

Today, Evangelist Tinuke has three children. She has dedicated herself to propagating the love and power of God as the Evangelism Coordinator of a popular Pentecostal Church in Nigeria.

In their home, Tinuke and her husband are growing more and more in love and their family unit is flourishing. All these blessings are attributed, by Evangelist Tinuke, to the power of prayers. She says, *"Anything that must die in me or outside my life for me to see the glory of God must die, notwithstanding the cost."*

Life lesson 71: Evidence is the end of explanation!

Revelation is the birth-place
for revival and revolution.

Chapter Seventy-two

John Kohlenberger: A meteorite with trailblazing revelation!

"Although the fig tree shall not blossom, neither shall fruit be in the vines; the labor of the olive shall fail, and the fields shall yield no meat; the flock shall be cut off from the fold, and there shall be no herd in the stalls: Yet I will rejoice in the Lord, I will joy in the God of my salvation" (Habakkuk 3:17-18).

John Kohlenberger III (1951 – 2015) was a Bible scholar par excellence. In the words of Dr. Gundry, the Vice President and Editor in Chief of his publisher Zondervan, *"John's contributions to Christian publishing, Bible publishing and Bible reference tools are without equal in his generation."*

His legacy of scholarly work includes the *NIV Exhaustive Concordance*, cross-references currently used in all NIV Bibles, the *Greek-English New Testament: UBS fifth Revised Edition* (NIV), and *the Inter-Linear NIV Hebrew-English Old Testament* amidst several others.

He began publishing these works while still obtaining his Masters degree from seminary at the tender age of twenty-five. Even though he never went on to obtain a Doctorate in Theology, his legacy of tools for Bible study are worth more than several Doctorates put together.

He wrote for the lay reader and gave, through his thirty-two seminal works, access to seminary-like Greek and Hebrew lectures for the interested but non-Bible-School-trained individual. He defined his life purpose as that of a map-guide that helped people get from one point to the other using the word of God.

He attended Multnomah Bible College in Oregon, and was a best-selling author several times over for his scholastic work. He married his childhood sweetheart, Carolyn, and they had two children – Josh and Sarah – who gave them four grandchildren.

Prostrate in worship in spite of his prostate!

In 2002, doctors gave John two to three years to live after having diagnosed him with metastatic prostate cancer. He lived thirteen years instead and continued writing through the pain and turmoil of chemotherapy, radiation therapy and hormonal therapy.

In October 2015, however, John's fight with cancer was over. He died after a gallant fight and with an unwavering faith. He left a rich heritage of faith-building resources that has changed a generation, equipped the church and revealed hitherto-concealed Hebrew and Greek secrets to a new collection of Word-of-God-Bible-perusing Christians.

In fact, he wrote more scholarly works and, according to his personal testimony, discovered more of God's love and faithfulness in the midst of his challenges. He tells of writing through unrestrained pain, and never complaining because the love of God was so real to him.

Life lesson 72: Life is not measured by its duration, but its donation to eternal causes

*If the devil can distract you,
then he can destroy you*

- Dr. Paul Enenche
(Snr. Pastor Dunamis International
Gospel Center, Abuja, Nigeria)

Chapter Seventy-three

Heidi's husband's healing

"If thou wilt diligently hearken to the voice of the LORD thy God, and wilt do that which is right in his sight, and wilt give ear to his commandments, and keep all his statutes, I will put none of these diseases upon thee, which I have brought upon the Egyptians: for I am the LORD that healeth thee" (Exodus 15:26).

Rolland Baker is the behind-the-scenes leader of Iris Ministries and the husband of maverick healing missionary and teacher Heidi Baker. Together, they have seen God set up more than 10,000 satellite bush churches in Mozambique through their ministry. He has also caused their ministry to impact a country that at the beginning of their outreach in 1995, was classified as the poorest nation on earth.

He and his wife were married in their early twenties and started a drama and music ministry in Indonesia before relocating their ministry base to Pemba, Mozambique, in 1995. They started by taking over an indolent and run-down orphanage near Maputo, Mozambique, and brought in hundreds of orphaned children to experience the love of God.

Notwithstanding communist and corrupt government policies, they thrived and have impacted a generation of Mozambique citizens with the gospel. They build water wells, feed the poor, care for the sick, educate the impoverished, start Bible schools and preach the gospel with signs and wonders following.

Virtual reality!

The Bakers have *"always gone out on a limb expecting God to show up"* according to Professor Candy Brown of Indiana University School of Religious Studies. However, nothing stretched their faith more than the sudden disease that afflicted Rolland while living in the hinterland of Mozambique in 2005.

The night before Rolland became ill, he had a dream where a demonic spirit from the Middle East came to destroy him - as an entry point to pull down Iris ministries. Within twenty-four hours, Rolland was paralyzed in his lower limbs and unable to wear his trousers or button a shirt. He lost his memory completely and doctors diagnosed him with vascular dementia exacerbated by cerebral malaria.

These physicians called Heidi, Rolland's wife, and told her to call her children to see their father for the last time. They envisaged he had less than thirty days to live and would never regain recognition of his environment. Throughout this ordeal, Heidi kept ministering to the over ten thousand orphans in Iris children's Centers flung out over 20 countries. She refused to believe the report of the doctors as reality.

Heidi Baker was approached by friends in Germany who heard about Rolland's plight, and they offered to pay for his care in a Christian-care community center in Germany. At this facility, he was seen by different physicians who prayed for him, treated him with medications but also altered his nutritional package.

Within three months, he was fully recovered and his memory regained its full cognitive function. He was retested severally in United States of America and Africa, but not a trace of dementia was found! He has since regained normal physical and psychological function, and was even able to apply and obtain his United States pilot's license.

God healed Ronnie because that was his virtual reality! After his healing, he testified that even though he could not do anything for himself in his bout with dementia, he never ceased praying. He continued in the one thing that will never change - the Word of God - and triumphed in faith as a result.

Life lesson 73: Never Give up because unbelief always ends in ignominy.

It is the Spirit of Faith that makes or breaks a man or woman!

Chapter Seventy-four

The 40ᵗʰ Birthday surprise

"Now unto him that is able to do exceeding abundantly above all that we ask or think, according to the power that worketh in us" (Ephesians 3:20).

Mrs. Aly was in her late thirties and had one child – an adorable ten-year old female. She wanted another child and was trusting God for the fruit of the womb, but for more than ten years had tried without success.

As she neared forty, her expectation began to ebb. She really did want another child; but according to her gynecologist, it would be risky for her and the baby. Based on her age biologically, she was told repeatedly that it was impossible for her to conceive as she had run out of eggs with which to conceive.

To her astonishment, however, and to the glory of God, she found out she was pregnant after her fortieth birthday. The doctors were shocked, but Aly and her husband were elated. The delivery was complicated by pre-eclampsia, and she had to be put on strict bedrest for the last six months of the pregnancy.

At 41 years of age, Aly welcomed her bundle of joy into the world. He was an answer to the prayers of a fervent mother. Today, this boy is almost six years old and growing *"...in wisdom, stature and in favor with God and with man"* (Luke 2:52).

Marriage, Motherhood and Ministry!

After training two children in the Lord up to school age, Aly wanted to do more for God's ministry. She joined the Assembly, West Monroe, and alongside her husband opened their home to a Friday night prophetic service in Tallulah, Louisiana.

They saw accelerated revival in their home which spurred Aly to adventure into the nearby women's prison as a chaplain. Currently, she serves as the chaplain to more than six hundred women in a women-only facility in Louisiana and brings God's deliverance to these women through the power in the word of God.

Her home is, however, her first ministry station. She never ceases to revel in how God gave her their family's own "Isaac" against all odds. She has faced several odds, some spiritual, and others marital or physical but through it all Aly has made a covenant to serve God whatever happens.

Life Lesson 74: Your loyalty to the King determines His lethality to your enemies.

It is your determination that decides the delivery of your deliberations and desires!

Chapter Seventy-five

John Hagee,
A Modern Day Moses

"...by a prophet the Lord *brought Israel out of Egypt, and*
by a prophet was he preserved" (Hosea 12:13).

Pastor John Hagee is the chairman of Christians United For Israel (CUFI), the largest pro-Israel support group in the world.
He is also the senior pastor of Cornerstone Church, and chief executive of Global Evangelism Television all in San Antonio, Texas, United States of America (USA).

He has blazed a trail in contemporary ministry with his cutting-edge incendiary sermons that have reawakened America to the ideals of the founding fathers of America. His congregation of over 25,000 is one of the largest in the USA and he has, also, pioneered landmark programs including a *"Night to Honor Israel."*

He has crossed generational, racial and denominational barriers to impact the modern-day church. Today, he is a rallying point for younger preachers who want to succeed in ministry.

He was in 1971 targeted by an incensed husband who, at point-blank range and in the middle of the Wednesday mid-week service, shot John Hagee six times. With only his Bible to protect him, John Hagee raised it up to heaven and none of the bullets touched him.

From Hawaii with hoarseness

While preaching in Maui, Hawaii in 2014, John Hagee noticed he was mispronouncing words and had a hard time forming the words in his mind. He quickly closed the service and returned to San Antonio, Texas. On arrival, he went through a battery of tests and finally the diagnosis of myasthenia Gravis was made. The doctors said he may never preach again and, definitely that he would be unable to play his highly beloved saxophone.

They also placed him on total voice rest for two weeks, started various medications and began speech and physical therapy on John Hagee to enable him regain some level of verbal and physical function. Meanwhile, all this time the devil was telling him that the Television ministry was over and he would never preach again. He rejected this satanic assertion and chose to rather believe the report of the Lord!

In the following weeks, John Hagee received eighty hours of intravenous treatment that pushed his human body to the outer edges of human endurance. It made him vomit and sapped strength out of his body completely, but he refused to discontinue the treatment that continued between June and September 2014.

In those stormy days, John Hagee cast his cares upon the Lord in prayer. He slowly regained function, and the doctors told him not to stand while preaching but sit behind a desk to preach. By December 2014, however, John Hagee was playing his saxophone and preaching all over the world without restraint.

His rheumatologist, Dr. Jackson, described him as "her miracle." Today at seventy-six years of age after open-heart bypass surgery, two knee replacement surgeries and now myasthenia Gravis, John Hagee is angling for more preaching time with his son, Matthew Hagee, who is the executive pastor of Cornerstone Church.

Life lesson 75: Always doubt your doubts, and fight for your faith because faith always wins!

> *The devil is not only on a watch, but is also on a leech. He is withheld from touching God's anointed!*
>
> **- Pastor Shane Warren**
> **(The Assembly, West Monroe, Louisiana, USA)**

Chapter Seventy-six

Chrissy Cymbala: A turn-around testimony

"For all the promises of God in him are yea, and in him Amen, unto the glory of God by us" (2 Corinthians 1:20).

C arol and Jim Cymbala pastor the world-famous Brooklyn Tabernacle Church and Choir in Brooklyn, New York. Their daughter, Chrissy had always been a model child; but, to her parents' dismay, at the age of sixteen she had a child out of wedlock. At eighteen, she moved out of the house and moved in with a man who was almost twice her age.

Her parents were distraught but not deterred. They maintained a testimony of faith with Carol Cymbala composing her famous hymn *"He Has Been Faithful to Me"* in the throes of the two-and-a-half-year crises. Chrissie refused all their overtures, rejected counseling from seasoned Christian counselors and started using drugs and alcohol.

Then, one night during a church prayer meeting, a female church member sent Pastor Cymbala a note saying, *"I feel impressed that we should stop the meeting and all pray for your daughter."* Pastor Cymbala complied, and heaven rose up in attention as the whole church prayed for Chrissie.

Forever yes!

Within forty-eight hours, Chrissy had reaffirmed her faith in Christ. She had had a dream that same Tuesday night of a deep abyss that never seemed to end and of God's protecting her from it. She literally ran to her parents' house, repented, and asked for their forgiveness. She lay on the floor of her parents' kitchen that Thursday evening and asked her dad only one question. She asked, *"who was praying for me on Tuesday night?*

Her parents responded, *"the whole church was praying for you Tuesday night."* According to Pastor Cymbalta, the prayers of the Church that night were akin to a woman delivering a new born baby and surely it gave birth to Chrissy spiritually. After graduating in flying colors from Bible school, Chrissy entered ministry, married a pastor and is today a Pastor's wife, worship leader and mother of three lovely children.

Her story is chronicled in her recent book *Girl in the Song* as an inspiration to parents and teenagers of God's redeeming love. Her experience left an enduring lesson for Jim and Carol Cymbala which they have never forgotten: it is with God all things are possible if persistent prayer is continually applied and faith always says, *"Yea and Amen."*

Life Lesson 76: One moment with God is greater than a lifetime with men.

*If God assists you, no man
or devil can resist you!*

Chapter Seventy-seven

The girl kidnapped at Winners Chapel, Lagos

"And Jesus increased in wisdom and stature, and in favor with God and man" (Luke 2:52).

Baby Praise Eleng was two years old when she was kidnapped on April 17, 2011, in the children's department of Winner's Chapel, Otta, near Lagos, Nigeria. Her parents, Mr. and Mrs. Samuel Eleng, were devastated; and the church was perplexed at how she could have disappeared from their iron-cast security.

The Church, Winner's chapel, is the largest church building in the world and it has a congregation greater than three hundred thousand members. The Church immediately sent out a message to the police who combed the surrounding areas for upward to two years without fruition.

The Bishop of the church, David Oyedepo, PhD, however, refused to be discouraged. He told the parents their daughter would be found and they should keep their hope and faith alive in God. The media were awash with all kinds of possible permutations surrounding little Praise's whereabouts, but God had an ace up His sleeve.

Three abductions later

In June 2013, Benjamin Ajaelu came to Winner's Chapel, Lagos, demanding to speak to Bishop David Oyedepo. He said he had kidnapped Baby Praise Eleng two years previously, and sold her to a woman for one hundred dollars in the city of Kano, in northern Nigeria.

The kidnapper reminisced to the Bishop how he had been having nightmares since he had kidnapped the girl. He was also fast going blind and dying from an unknown disease. He was then led to the congregation at Winner's Chapel, Lagos where he made his confession public.

The Police then arrested Mr. Ajaelu, and with his help, traced Baby Praise Eleng to Enugu, Nigeria. The woman who had bought her in 2011, while she resided in Kano, Nigeria had sold her to another woman in Enugu for an undisclosed sum. By this time, Baby Praise was four years old and the Police had closed her case considering her dead or forever lost.

A few days after his confession to the police, Mr. Ajaelu died but he had left enough information for the police to track Baby Praise's current abductor. The woman who had bought her from Mr. Ajaelu, and the woman who currently had custody of Baby Praise were arrested and incarcerated in Enugu, Nigeria. Thankfully, Baby Praise was hale and hearty.

Baby Praise's mother and father were ecstatic. They said, amidst tears, "I bless the name of the Lord! God is awesome. I thought my waiting was in vain. But I have now seen the hand of God. I will serve God all the days of my life." While the criminals were arrested, the parents celebrated the recovery of their precious daughter.

Life Lesson 77: Fear burdens, but faith bulldozes!

Don't let the world tell you what you can't do. Tell them, instead, what God can do!

Chapter Seventy-eight

Mariah Todd: Bred in fire and Birthed by Faith!

"If you have faith like a grain of mustard seed, you shall say to this mountain be thou removed and it shall move" (Mark 11:22).

Evangelist Tim Todd and his wife, Angie, are pillars of the church in West Monroe, Louisiana. They are vision-coordinators of the *"Revival Fires"* worldwide ministry and have taken the gospel to all major continents of the world. They broadcast on radio all over the world, and have developed a free Bible resource called "Truth for Youth" Bible that has impacted millions of youth internationally.

They have four children, including twins - Mariah and Miracle Joy - who are a testimony to the power of God to overcome evil medical diagnosis. These twins overcame twin-to-twin transfusion syndrome at birth and have grown to become undergraduates at School of Urban Missions Bible College in West Monroe, Louisiana.

The Todds' faith was further tested in early 2015 when Mariah, still in her late teens, began complaining of increasing weakness and worsening neck swelling. They took her to an Otolaryngologist in the community who ordered a fine needle aspiration of the thyroid. The results returned, to the dismay of all involved, as high grade follicular cancer of the thyroid.

From Recovery to Results!

The diagnosis was devastating to Mariah and her family. They had, however, overcome death following the twin-to-twin transfusion syndrome that bedeviled the twins at birth and knew Mariah was a candidate for God's miracle.

The local otolaryngologist referred her to a specialist in Georgia, USA who scheduled her for a surgical procedure called total thyroidectomy. The church in West Monroe, Louisiana and friends of the Todd family who knew about Mariah, raised up a hedge of prayer around her as she went in for surgery.

The surgery was uneventful and deemed successful by the surgical team. According to the surgeon, if they had waited any further the cancer would have spread to other parts of her body. On excision of the thyroid, it was observed that the follicular cancer in it was contained within the thyroid. Today, Mariah is a cancer free bubbly and energetic woman of God.

Life Lesson 78: What satan uses to silence you, God turns around to make you succeed!

If you don't face your enemy, he will phase you out in stages!

Chapter Seventy-nine

The Apostle of Always Joy

"For the kingdom of God is not meat and drink; but righteousness, and peace, and joy in the Holy Ghost. For he that in these things serveth Christ is acceptable to God, and approved of men" (Romans 14:17-18).

Pastor (Dr) Joy Dara is the pastor of the largest church in central Louisiana. He arrived America in 1980 as an undergraduate student, and had to sleep on classroom floors because of limited resources.

As a Christian, however, he believed in always being joyful regardless of the circumstance. His philosophy of life stems from James 1:2-4 which says, *"...count it all joy when ye fall into divers temptations. Knowing this, that the trying of your faith works patience. But let patience have her perfect work, that ye may be perfect and entire wanting nothing."*

He excelled in his classroom studies and went on to obtain a Doctor of Jurisprudence (JD) degree from Southern University, Baton Rouge, Louisiana, and Masters of Law degree from the University of Arkansas, Fayetteville, after his Bachelor of Arts degree from California Baptist University, Riverside.

From glory to glory

As a minister, he served under different denominational leaders as worship leader and assistant pastor. He married, had children; and as he settled into secular life, was invited by a local church to serve as their pastor.

This church was not growing and had lost two pastors in under a year to mysterious circumstances. The church board that interviewed him pointedly asked him, *"Do you still want the job knowing the previous two occupants died suddenly?"*

In his ebullient and unassuming manner, Joy Dara said that he was not afraid of death; and if given the position, he would cause that spirit of death to depart from the church. He took the position as senior pastor and in less than ten years the church increased in leaps and bounds.

The congregation built a state of the art facility that seats over a thousand people, anchored a international television program called "Always Joy" and attracted respect from the community with their innovative programs designed to empower the local population.

Dr. Joy Dara currently oversees hundreds of inter-denominational ministers and his influence is felt across race, denomination and age. He has been fondly called the apostle of always Joy!

Life Lesson 79: We cannot all do great things, but we can all do small things with great love.

God hid you in Him so
satan can't find you!

Chapter Eighty

Shane Warren: From Heart Patient to Healthy Pops!

"O God, my heart is fixed; I will sing and give praise, even with my glory. Awake, psaltery and harp: I myself will awake early" (Psalm 108:1-2).

Pastor Shane Warren is the lead Pastor at The Assembly West Monroe, Louisiana. He has transformed, through the anointing of the Holy Ghost, a monolithic and predominantly Caucasian congregation into a multiracial and economically pluralistic church with diverse ethnic groups in less than ten years.

He and his wife, Pam Warren, moved to West Monroe, Louisiana in 2007 and began as senior pastor of a deeply divided church of less than one hundred and fifty people. The church had undergone leadership resignations that led to at least three groups of members leaving the parent church – First Assembly West Monroe, Louisiana – and starting their own congregations in the Monroe/West Monroe area.

In pursuit of his vision to restore the glory and revive the parent church that was tottering on its precipice, Pastor Shane embarked on radical ventures in the community. This included buying a Christian Television station, opening the first full-gospel charismatic Bible school in the area and opening a branch of the church in the inner city of Monroe designed to reach that community. He also began a new building project for the church that would seat two thousand people with state of the art facilities.

Fulfilled, fun-filled and filled with the Holy Ghost

As Pastor Shane embarked on and executed these multimillion dollar projects, their stress began to take a toll on his health. He became unusually tired, and after trying several energy-boosting formulas, he presented to the Emergency Room with chest pain, shortness of breadth and dyspnea on exertion.

The cardiologists diagnosed him with irregular heart rate and promptly placed a pacemaker to regulate his heart beat. He was discharged from the hospital, but he was soon admitted again. This time he underwent a Percutaneous Coronary Intervention (PCI) which showed multiple blockages in several major arteries.

According to his cardiologists, he would never be able to preach again as the strain of energetic speaking would be too much pressure for his heart. He was subsequently placed on multiple heart medications, and as a consequence of these new medications Pastor Shane reported repeated dizziness, heart burn and even outright bleeding.

The preacher in Pastor Shane would, however, not be silenced. He continued to minister but with less fervor and vigor than was characteristic. Eventually, he underwent a surgical procedure that enabled him to lose hundreds of pounds of weight. As a result, he has gotten off all his medications and is healthier than ever.

To crown this transition, from heart patient to healthy pastor, Pastor Shane and Pam watched as their only child, Adam, got married in May 2016. It was a dream come true for them, but a dream only God could have made possible as the males in Pastor Shane's family had repeatedly suffered premature death. Pastor Shane today is a healthy pops-to-be, as his son and daughter-in-law are expecting his first grandchild.

Life Lesson 80: What God quickens, nobody can quench!

Soon is God's signature, not later!

Chapter Eighty-one

From Bakavu to Breakthrough

"...God hath chosen the foolish things of the world to confound the wise; and God hath chosen the weak things of the world to confound the things which are mighty; And base things of the world, and things which are despised, hath God chosen, yea, and things which are not, to bring to nought things that are: That no flesh should glory in his presence" (1 Corinthians 1:27-28).

Mr. Richard was in the last day of his death row sentence at the famed Bakavu Prison in Congo, Africa. He had been convicted of murdering a man in self-defense and had been imprisoned in the ramshackle, make-shift prison while waiting for the execution of his death sentence by hanging.

On the penultimate day before his execution, Evangelist Reinhard Boonke visited the prison. It was 1989, and the world-renowned evangelist was in Bakavu for a crusade. As he was being shown around the city by his ministry's field evangelist, he was taken to the local prison where the Christ For all Nation (CFaN) team had began a Bible study amongst the inmates.

As he entered the prison, Reinhard Bonnke heard praise and worship coming from Richard's cell. The sound of worship Evangelist Bonnke heard was being made by prisoners in shackles and behind iron bars. Among the about forty men in a sordid prison cell littered with filth and vermin, Reinhard noticed Richard with his missing front tooth and badly mangled limbs leading worship. At that time, the Holy Spirit spoke to Evangelist Bonnke saying, *"tell that man that he shall be free and become a preacher."*

Today, you are a free man!

When Reinhard Bonnke approached Richard and told him what the Spirit of God had just said, Richard turned to Evangelist Bonnke and said in the local Congolese dialect, *"The prison executioner comes daily. On the last two executions, I have been scheduled to be executed by hanging, but the executioner was fatigued. In fact, he told me I would be the first on the next execution day."* Reinhard Bonnke told him, *"God spared you to preserve your life. Just believe."*

As he went back to praising God with his fellow prisoners, Reinhard Bonnke went to his crusade contemplating how God was going to deliver Richard. Everything in Richard's life looked contrary to God's promise, but Reinhard and Richard held unto God's word.

After the crusade, Reinhard Bonnke went to the city official's house and pled for Richard. He met a city official's wife, who rather than help Richard to be released, asked Reinhard Bonnke for a bribe. The evangelist refused and walked away telling the official's wife, *"Richard is called to be a preacher; Don't stand in his way!"*

Twelve Years Later

In 2001, Reinhard Boonke was preaching in Kinshasha, Congo. After his miracle crusade ended, his evangelistic director told him there was someone he would like him to meet. He took Evangelist Bonnke to the back of the crusade stand where a black gentleman, with a gold tooth and wearing a maroon suit was standing.

As Reinhard Bonnke approached him, the man fell at his feet thanking him profusely. As he stood up, Evangelist Bonnke struggled to recall where he had known him. When the man said *"Bakuva,"* Reinhard Bonnke exclaimed *"Richard."*

Apparently, Richard had been released miraculously soon after the word of the Lord from Evangelist Bonnke came. He had become one of the sponsors of the Christ For all Nations Kinshasha, Congo, crusade which Reinhard Bonnke was headlining. His life had been transformed miraculously by that prison visit. Today, Richard is a preacher of the gospel!

Life Lesson 81: Walk with God, and you will never need to run after men.

Your environment
determines your element!

Chapter Eighty-two

Rod Parsley: From Silent to Silent No More!

"...he cast out the spirits with his word, and healed all that were sick: That it might be fulfilled which was spoken by Esaias the prophet, saying, Himself took our infirmities, and bare our sicknesses" (Matthew 8:16-17).

Rod Parsley is an apostle of the faith who has ministered in the capacity of an apostle, prophet, pastor, evangelist and teacher for more than forty years. He is the senior pastor of the World Harvest Church, Columbus, Ohio, and the president of Valor Christian College and Bridge of Hope Humanitarian Services.

He has helped shape the twentieth and twenty-first century church with his authentic gospel and ever-pioneering preaching. For example, he went to South Sudan and began freeing Christians who were enslaved to their Islamic captors by paying their captors thousands of dollars.

The annual world harvest convention, organized by the local church he superintends, has ministered to thousands across the world with a relevant word for today. He has built bridges across races in his local congregation, and his cutting-edge messages are heard in over 200 countries of the world and reach a potential audience of nearly two billion people weekly.

His greatest allotment in life and ministry, however, is being married to Joni for nearly forty years and raising two Godly children, Austin and Ashton. These two children work in the ministry, alongside their parents, and act as a bastion of faith for thousands of pastor's families who want the kind of ministry and family Rod and Joni Parsley have come to exemplify.

Squamous cell cancer shattered by radiation and relentless faith

In May 2015, because of a recalcitrant sore throat, Rod went to see his family physician who prescribed some anti-allergy and antibiotic medications for him. He, however, still had a harsh dryness in his throat. After a few months of persistent coughing and painful swallowing, his family physician referred him to an otolaryngologist.

The otolaryngologist decided to scope Rod Parsley's larynx. After the scope, a diagnosis of squamous cell carcinoma of the larynx was made. As someone who makes a living with his voice, he was advised to stop preaching immediately and undergo months of radiation therapy. Rod Parsley was shocked, and readily decided to doubt his doubts and feed his faith. As a result of this resolve, he kept the news to only his inner circle.

The radiation therapy affected his skin and made him unable to utter a sentence, but notwithstanding Rod continued to say soft prayers to God under his breadth. Throughout his radiation therapy, he kept saying, *"Tomorrow will be better than today."* The devil, on the other hand, would come to him and tell him, *"The ministry is over and the television ministry is finished."*

Pastor Parsley nevertheless made a choice to believe God! He came into agreement with God's word that said Jesus took all our infirmities and sicknesses away by His stripes, and by October 2015 Rod Parsley was declared cancer free. He was back preaching again by November 2015, and has not stopped since!

Life Lesson 82: If God can't do it, then it shouldn't be done at all!

"God is so big, that if we're truly walking with Him, even the attacks of the enemy add to our life and only make us better"

- **Wendy Treat** (wife of Casey Treat, testifying to God's goodness through the thirty-six months ordeal of Casey's chemotherapy and treatment for Hepatitis C).

Chapter Eighty-three

Casey Treat:
Healed from Hepatitis C

"He who is loose and slack in his work is brother to him who is a destroyer and he who does not use his endeavors to heal himself is brother to him who commits suicide" (Proverbs 18:9 – Amplified classic edition).

C asey Treat is the Pastor of Christian Faith Center in Seattle, Washington. As a teenager, he was involved with drugs and alcohol and went to jail on several occasions for minor misdemeanors. One occasion, in particular, he remembers was when his father refused to bail him out of jail and so he had to face a lengthy sentence in prison.

At the trial, the judge chose not to throw away the key and put Casey in jail at the age of nineteen. Instead, he decided to give Casey another chance. He promised to keep Casey out of jail on only one condition: He must finish drug rehabilitation. Casey gladly accepted the deal and went to a drug rehab headed by a black man named Julian who had spent twenty-four years in jail.

This man mentored Casey like a father and showed him the unconditional love of God. He believed in Casey; and the result of such an effusion of love, turned Casey's heart over to Jesus. He entered Bible college, and thereafter met his wife-to-be Wendy on campus. After obtaining a Bachelors Degree in Ministry, at the age of Twenty-four, Casey started Christian Faith Center, Seattle with thirty-four people.

Troubled but triumphant

The family and the Ministry blossomed. Wendy gave birth to three children, and worked part-time. The church exploded such that Casey Treat had to open two campuses in the greater Seattle area and begin a building program for a new $40 million facility in 2003.

At about this time, Casey was processing a new life insurance policy; and while undergoing routine pre-requisite medical tests. It was discovered that he had Hepatitis C. A chronic disease, Hepatitis C has the ability to lie dormant for several years and it looked more than likely that Casey's lifestyle as a teen intravenous drug user was the culprit.

While he believed God for his healing, Casey opted for a holistic approach to how God would bring it about using Proverbs 18:9 as his foundation scripture. He underwent eleven to twelve months of antiviral treatment, even though the prognosis of complete cure with the anti-viral medication was only four percent. At the end of one month of treatment, Casey's viral load was zero but he persisted with the fatigue, nausea and weight loss his medications caused in order to fully see his liver restored.

Following a two-year serial laboratory follow-up, not a trace of hepatitis was found in Casey Treat's body. His doctor then told the insurance company to insure Casey saying "*You can insure Mr. Treat. He will die someday, but it won't be from Hepatitis.*' He was totally and functionally cured. Today, Casey continues to travel the world preaching the uncompromising word of God to a dead and dying world.

Life Lesson 83: Believers never beg, they only believe!

Fill God up with you are fed up with, and He will fill you to overflowing!

Chapter Eighty-four

Bishop Jones: From Healer to Healed!

"Surely he hath borne our griefs, and carried our sorrows yet we did esteem him stricken, smitten of God, and afflicted. But he was wounded for our transgressions, he was bruised for our iniquities: the chastisement of our peace was upon him; and with his stripes we are healed" (Isaiah 53:4-5).

Bishop Jones is the worldwide presiding Bishop of Living Gospel Church. He pioneered the outreach arm of the church as an assistant to the founding Bishop. He spearheaded the branching out of the ministry from California to the rest of the world. Today that effort is evidenced by numerous church plants in six states in the Union - Georgia, Texas, Louisiana, California, Pennsylvania, Florida – and internationally in the Barbados Islands.

Bishop Jones planted Churches where it seemed non-viable and they thrived. He depended on the Holy Spirit for direction and as a result of his outstanding successes was promoted to the position of Presiding Bishop after the founder died in 1991. His ministry has been characterized by the supernatural! He has moved over six times, from California to Texas and now Louisiana, with outstanding results.

He underwent eye surgery in 2010 by a California-based ophthalmologist. Even though it was routine surgery, and he had a less than one percent chance of going blind, the surgery failed and that was the end of Bishop Jones sight. He and the church were devastated but continued in the ministry nonetheless.

Two years later, Bishop Jones was faced with another disease that was life-modifying. He was diagnosed with End Stage Renal Disease (ESRD) and placed on thrice-a-week Hemo-dialysis. Notwithstanding his health challenges, however, Bishop Jones refused to lighten his schedule. He continued his global pastorate, accompanied by preaching and teaching all over the world, to the congregations of the Living Gospel Church.

One Miracle Kidney

In 2015, after three years of hemo-dialysis and five years of blindness, a member of the Living Gospel Church in California - Sister Cherrie - declared to the Church that God had told her to give one of her two kidneys to Bishop Jones.

Even though Sister Cherrie is married with three children, is in her fifties and from a foreign country, the Philippines, she and Bishop Jones had exactly the same blood type. Bishop Jones and the church gladly accepted the miracle kidney gift from Sister Cherrie, and in October 2015, the transplant procedure took place in Shreveport, Louisiana.

The donor and recipient did very well, and after a few days were discharged from the hospital. Within days they both returned to full stream activities. Bishop Jones is no longer on hemo-dialysis and even though he is still blind, the miracle kidney from Sister Cherrie has enabled him to devote more time to the ministry. He continues to live a life of compassion and is an example of humility, holiness and hard work to thousands of believers' around the world.

Life Lesson 84: When you fix your eyes on God, He fixes all other things that try to make you fixate on them.

*There is no life so scattered
or shattered or battered
that the grace of God cannot
gather back together again!*

- Dr. Paul Enenche
**(Snr. Pastor Dunamis International
Gospel Center, Abuja, Nigeria).**

Chapter Eighty-five

Is Anyone Dead Here?

"...as ye go, preach, saying, the kingdom of heaven is at hand.
Heal the sick, cleanse the lepers, raise the dead, cast out devils:
freely ye have received, freely give" (Matthew 10:7-8).

Benson Idahosa (1937-1996) was a pioneer of the gospel in Nigeria. He began his ministry in 1972, by planting the Church of God Mission International in Benin City, Nigeria, following a stint at Christ for the Nations as a Bible student under the tutelage of Gordon Lindsay.

He broke down the fear of the occult in the ancient Benin Kingdom, by building his church in the feared forests of the kingdom where no one was supposed to live, talk less thrive. He refused to shave his head, or sacrifice fetish offerings to idols, when a King in the royal kingdom died. He also instructed his members not to obey similar demands from the palace.

He envisaged a prosperous God, who wants to prosper His church, when it was still considered a taboo for the average Church member or pastor to drive even a bicycle. He was a shoe-shiner at the time, but he believed God could elevate his status. He surrendered his life to Christ as a teenager and, while attending an Assemblies of God Church in Benin City, began to make grandiose plans to go to Bible school and preach the gospel.

He asked his pastor, after a Sunday service, where the pastor had preached on raising the dead, *"Can I raise the dead?"* The Pastor answered, and said *"I have never raised the dead, but I believe you can."* Benson left the church that morning on his bicycle and began a four to six-hour circuitous journey asking everyone he met, *"Is anyone dead here?"*

Do Not Despise the Days of Small Beginnings!

As Benson went from house to house, at about 4 P.M. in front of a house, he met a teenage girl named Margaret (who would later become his wife) crying. She told him that her niece had died about 9 A.M. that day and that they were getting ready to take her to the burial grounds.

Benson got excited, to the utter dismay of Margaret. He then explained to her the reason for his excitement. He wanted to raise her niece, Irrua, from the dead and asked Margaret to take him to her dead niece. She was wrapped in a bag, about to be buried, as she had died earlier that day from complications arising from seizures.

Benson then prayed for her but without a response. He tried to repeat Jesus pattern in Mark 5:41 where he raised Jairus daughter from the dead by saying *"Talitha Cumi."* Next Idahosa asked the parents *"what is her name?"* He then said, *"Irrua, get up"* but to no avail.

On the third occasion, however, Benson called her spirit back into her body and before he could finish his prayers, her eyes had opened and she was fully comprehensible and ambulatory. He then asked her parents to feed her, and as he left their house exhilarated at what God had done, he continued to ask all around the city *"Is anyone dead here?"*

This singular encounter endeared him to Margaret; and after his Bible school training, they were married. Together, they started Church of God Mission in 1972 and built the first mega-church in Nigeria with thousands of church branches, tens of Bible schools, hundreds of educational institutions and the first Christian University in the country.

He is considered the doyen of Pentecostalism in Nigeria. Through his generosity, he mentored thousands of pastors many of whom he sponsored to the All Nations for Christ Bible School he started. He died in 1996, but his legacy lives on in the lives of those who encountered him and still encounter him through his university, school, hospitals, churches or sermons from the Idahosa World Outreach stable.

Life Lesson 85: Never despise the day of small beginnings!

A *generous life washes the feet of those who once nailed theirs!*

- Shane Warren
(Lead Pastor, The Assembly West Monroe, Louisiana)

Chapter Eighty-six

Lea Joyner: Pioneer Preacher and Martyred Minister!

"Except a corn of wheat fall into the ground and die, it abideth alone: but if it die, it bringeth forth much fruit. He that loveth his life shall lose it; and he that hateth his life in this world shall keep it unto life eternal" (John 12:24-25).

Lea Travis Joyner was born in Natchez, Mississippi on June 17, 1917. She attended elementary and high school in Grayson, Louisiana, and followed that with tertiary education at Westminster College, Tehuacana and High Point College in North Carolina.

On January 1, 1939 Rev. Lea Joyner was ordained as the first female United Methodist minister in the state of Louisiana. The church leadership sent her to Columbia district, Louisiana where she planted Columbia Heights Methodist Church. After five years in the saddle as pastor, she came to Monroe, Louisiana to assist Dr. Adrian Serex of the First Methodist church in Monroe.

Lea Joyner's dream as a teenager had been to be a missionary to India. She planted three churches – North Grand, South Grand and Gibson's chapel – while serving as Dr. Serex's assistant. Her missionary zeal eventually led her to establish a Methodist Church, on the Southside of the city called Southside United Methodist Church. It opened its doors to the public on July 13, 1952.

By the end of the first year, the new Southside Church had two hundred and thirty seven congregants. She encouraged education and helped in the training of more than nineteen members of her congregation for ministry positions. She built what many consider the first multiracial mega-church of her day in Louisiana.

After thirty-three years of serving them as pastor, Lea Joyner's congregation had swelled to more than two thousand congregants. She had an open-door policy, and welcomed all and sundry to her Church. She never married or had children but made her Southside community her family.

Breakthrough or Breakdown!

On March 11, 1985, an ex-convict and repeat offender Earl Eaton murdered Rev. Lea Joyner in cold blood. He had perpetrated a plan to steal Rev. Joyner's white Honda car and relocate with it to Florida. As Lea Joyner came out of her office at about 10:45 P.M. that night, Earl hit her on the head and pulled a blanket over her unconscious body.

He then stabbed her repeatedly - over thirty times - and dumped her body in a cotton field enroute to Arkansas. Forensic Pathology describes Lea Joyner's time of death as about one to two hours after her initial trauma to the head and most probably interspersed with aggravated rape by the assailant.

After tracking Earl down to his Aunt's house in Arkansas, the police arraigned and tried him for first degree murder. In its verdict, the Louisiana state Supreme Court sentenced him to death for first degree murder after an initial appeal by the defendant citing insanity was denied.

On the day of her burial, sixty-seven year old Lea Joyner was honored by thousands who came to pay their last respects. The city within a few months also paid their respects to this icon by renaming the Bridge linking West Monroe and Monroe and the express road in front of the Civic Center after her.

The legacy of Lea Joyner is still alive today! She opened the door for female ministers in the United Methodist Church of the Louisiana district and is credited with breaking down the walls of racism, social inequality and sexism in the Louisiana church of today.

Life Lesson 86: It is the donation of your life, not its duration, that counts!

God does not consult your past
to determine your future!

Chapter Eighty-seven

Tyler Cook: Delivered from drugs!

"And of his fulness have all we received, and grace for grace. For the law was given by Moses, but grace and truth came by Jesus Christ" (John 1:16-17).

T yler Cook was only sixteen years old when he first experimented with marijuana. As a gateway drug, that habit opened doors for other drugs such as cocaine, methamphetamine and heroine. As this habit progressed, Tyler's younger brother was diagnosed with a rare condition called clear cell carcinoma of the kidney and given less than a year to live.

Tyler felt a sense of disillusionment and despondency that caused his use of drugs to spiral even further out of control. As the senior brother and only sibling, Tyler was disconsolate and felt even more distanced from God as a result. To the utter despair of his parents, instead of turning to God, Tyler turned to drugs and alcohol for relief.

To stem this downward spiral, Tyler's parents arranged for him to relocate to an aunt's house in West Monroe, Louisiana. He had just graduated from high school, and his parents felt the streets of West Virginia were a negative influence on him.

On arrival in West Monroe, Louisiana, he continued his ungodly lifestyle. He had a praying aunt, however, who was attending a local church called the Assembly, West Monroe, at the time. She invited him, and on his parents urging, he agreed to attend.

God's Miraculous Arrest!

That Sunday morning service at the Assembly, West Monroe, Louisiana, was different. Instead of a traditional three-point sermon and altar call, the pastor interrupted the praise and worship service with an ardent cry.

The lead pastor of the Church, Shane Warren, declared that morning that there was someone in the congregation that God wanted to save and advised the individual to come to the altar. He said that God had told him this someone needed to make a life-altering decision immediately. As a result of his being pre-occupied by this urgent matter, Pastor Shane declared that he had been unable to sleep for four days!

He asked, again, that whomever he was addressing step out. As the Church went into a time of prayer, Tyler Cook walked forward sobbing, shaking uncontrollably and full of Godly sorrow. He dropped to his knees at the altar, and cried out to God for forgiveness repenting truly of his sins. That day in 2010, Tyler was saved, delivered from drugs and filled with the Holy Ghost.

Today, six years later, Tyler is a graduate of the School of Urban Missions Bible School, and the Junior High Ministry Pastor at the Assembly, West Monroe, Louisiana. He is also the devoted husband of Kristen. He has metamorphosed from a habitual drug user who didn't want anything to do with Church, to a spiritual aphrodisiac who can't seem to go without Church for any period of time.

Life lesson 87: Those who are broken by God are unbreakable when faced with indomitable odds!

> # "My words in My mouth are as powerful as My words in your mouth"
>
> ### - God's word to Evangelist Reinhard Bonnke when he was not seeing miracles in his ministry

Chapter Eighty-eight

Pastor Foster: Healed by the blood of Jesus!

"For as much then as the children are partakers of flesh and blood, he also himself likewise took part of the same; that through death he might destroy him that had the power of death, that is, the devil; And deliver them who through fear of death were all their lifetime subject to bondage" (Hebrews 2:14-15).

Pastor Mark Foster is a second generation preacher, who took over the pastorate of the Pentecostals West Monroe, Louisiana from his father in 1996. He has been married for forty-five years to the love of his life, Paula Adams Foster and they have two sons, four granddaughters and one grandson.

Apart from his role as pastor, Mark serves as chaplain of the West Monroe High School football team and the Ouachita Parish Sheriffs' mounted patrol. He serves by appointment of the governor, on the Louisiana Children's Trust Fund Board and is a founding member of Community Prayer Partners of the Twin Cities. He has served as Youth President, Home Missions Director, and Presbyter in North Carolina and also served as Home Missions Director in the Southeast Region and General Home Missions Secretary for the United Pentecostal Church International.

He is considered an elder statesman of the Church in Louisiana and has contributed to establishing the church in the West Monroe/

Monroe area as a formidable force with which to contend. As lead Pastor of the Pentecostals Church in West Monroe, he has seen explosive growth spiritually, numerically and property wise. He took over a church in the hundreds, but today the Pentecostals of West Monroe sit on the I-20 Highway, uses state of the art facilities and accommodates upward of a thousand members who attend its three weekend services.

Nothing Missing!

In 2010, however, Pastor Mark Foster received devastating news. He had stage three colon cancer and would most likely not live beyond one year. He went to Mayo Clinic, Rochester, for chemo-radiation treatment and a second opinion on the viability of surgery.

He started medications for cancer, and within one year he was declared cancer free. Since the initial treatment in 2010, Pastor Foster has travelled annually to Mayo Clinic, Rochester, Minnesota, for follow up. On each visit, he has been given a clean bill of health.

In spite of his health challenges, Pastor Mark continues to preach and lead the church with ardent worship and trail-blazing messages from God. He has preached across denominational lines, and enjoys building relationships across race and societal class lines with like-minded individuals. His life is a testimony of God's power, purity and passion.

Life Lesson 88: One with God is majority!

Acceleration without direction is frustration!

Chapter Eighty-nine

Gary Bentley:
From Zero to Hero

*"He restoreth my soul: he leadeth me in the paths of
righteousness for his name's sake"* (Psalm 23:3).

G ary Bentley is the State Director for Louisiana Teen Challenge.
He and his wife Pat have worked tirelessly over the last twenty
years to see individuals who were addicted to drugs, alcohol
or some other maleficent lifestyle restored to a life of faith in Christ
with power to live victoriously.

Gary himself went to Teen Challenge in 1997, after a stint in prison
for alcoholism and driving while intoxicated. Even though he was
from a middle-class family with church roots, he had battled cocaine,
alcohol and pornographic addiction for eighteen years. In a bid to
stem the drift, his family had sent him to five different secular drug
rehabilitation programs but all to no avail.

At the age of thirty-three, he was sentenced to jail for forging
checks. After three years in jail, he was released to the streets of New
Orleans. Now divorced and homeless, Gary returned to alcoholism and
illicit drug use. He was soon arrested by the police for malfeasance
behavior associated with repeated drug and alcohol use.

While in that New Orleans Jail, Gary got a Bible from the Gideon's
Bible Ministry. After reading the gospel of John, he surrendered his

life to Christ and immediately lost the desire for cigarettes and illicit drugs. Miraculously, at about the same time Gary was dedicating his life to Christ, his mother in Alabama was standing in for him at an altar call and believing God for his ultimate restoration!

Restoration not rehabilitation

Gary Bentley's mother, unaware of what God had done in his life, relayed the phone number for New Orleans Teen Challenge which her pastor had given her, to him. On his release from jail, Gary walked fifteen miles to New Orleans Teen Challenge. He had been delivered from the *spirit of pharmakeia* but he needed to learn how to continue in true Christ-bought freedom.

Teen challenge, founded by David Wilkerson in the 1950's, was unique in that they had a spirit-filled rehabilitation curriculum with a ninety-seven percent success rate. Gary spent one year in the Teen Challenge drug rehab program, and afterwards continued as an employee. He has been clean and off alcohol and drugs for more than twenty years and is currently the chief operating officer for Louisiana Teen Challenge. He oversees a twelve million dollar budget and facilitates the discipleship of over two hundred men and women annually who want to undergo a Christ-centered drug rehabilitation program.

In 1998 he married Pat, a nurse, and today they are happily married with three lovely daughters. He has mentored and inspired thousands of men and women for Christ and has supervised the planting of Teen Challenge offices in Russia and in the former Eastern Bloc nations.

Life lesson 89: Rehab is going back to what you used to be but restoration is going back to what God has called you to be!

I have no Plan B when God has given me his plan A

- Carman Licciaredell
Music producer, praise and worship singer

Chapter Ninety

Carman: Back from the dead

"But if the Spirit of him that raised up Jesus from the dead dwell in you, he that raised up Christ from the dead shall also quicken your mortal bodies by his Spirit that dwelleth in you" (Romans 8:11).

O n January 14, 2013, Carman otherwise known as Carmelo Domenic Licciardello announced to a worldwide audience that he had been diagnosed with multiple myeloma and had been given less than three years to live. He sent out prayer requests to his numerous followers in the gospel music industry and church family scene. As a result, thousands of prayers went up around the world for Carman.

As a Christian pop icon, Carman had blazed a trail in contemporary urban gospel music that was unprecedented. He had filled a Texas stadium with more than 71,000 people for a Christian concert which is still recorded as the largest gathering for a music concert in American history. He has recorded more than fifteen platinum and gold albums, and sold more than ten million albums to this date.

An avowed reformer, Carman raised more than $300,000.00 from his sick bed with the intention of organizing one hundred "No Plan B" concerts all over America. He had gone through several near-death experiences during his chemotherapy treatment, lost all his hair as a result but never became angry or belligerent toward God.

Melanoma: Just another word!

After Carman's doctors told him he had just three years to live, he told the saints, "*The devil has put cancer on the wrong Italian.*" He believed the report of the Lord that God could restore the years the locusts have eaten away and give peace and confidence when everyone else is losing their minds.

He challenged believers to believe God to the uttermost. He quoted repeatedly from Mark 16:18, saying, "*...they* (believers) *shall lay hands on the sick, and they shall recover.*" He advocated for believers to use medicine, trust God and maintain a healthy diet and do regular exercise.

Today, Carman is cancer-free. He has no trace of multiple myeloma in his body, according to his doctors. He is an evidence of the power of God, and the authority in the name of Jesus. He headlined a nationwide "Victory Tour" where at the end of each concert he prays for the sick and hopeless and sees God's resurrection power flow miraculously.

Life Lesson 90: What the devil thinks is your end is a bend to take you to your next wind!

There is no mountain anywhere, but every man or woman's ignorance is his or her own mountain!

- Bishop David Oyedepo
(Presiding Bishop, Living Faith Church Worldwide)

Chapter Ninety-one

David Oyedepo:
Healed from tuberculosis

"...how God anointed Jesus of Nazareth with the Holy Ghost and power and He went about doing good and healing all that were oppressed of the devil (Acts 10:38).

D avid Oyedepo is a general in today's generation for Christ. He has fought the Northern Nigerian Islamic hegemonic oligarchy that has sought to prevent Christian penetration of Northern Nigeria. He has, also, broken barriers to Church ownership in the North and braved odds to establish the Living Faith Church as one of the largest Christian organizations in the world with over five thousand branches of the ministry across the globe.

He gave his life to Christ as a young sixteen-year-old high school student, after hearing the gospel from his erstwhile American born missionary teacher Ms. Betty Lasher. He had been brought up in a part Animist, Moslem and nominal Christian family, and after hearing the gospel from his teacher, turned fully toward Christ. He began preaching aggressively and within a space of five years was a well-known speaker on the campus circuit in Ilorin, Nigeria.

After graduating from college in 1981 as an architect, David Oyedepo went on to launch the Living Faith foundation. This Church, commonly called Winner's chapel today, in currently in over thirty-five countries of the world. It is at the forefront of transforming Africa, as a continent through the African Gospel Invasion Project (AGIP).

He is currently the proprietor of two Universities, Landmark and Covenant Universities, numerous elementary and high schools and has published more than seventy books which have all together sold greater than four million copies. He has also commissioned the construction of five additional universities in other countries

Tuberculosis Destroyed

In September 1969, David Oyedepo woke up one night and discovered that his dormitory mates had moved away from his space because he coughed very badly with blood-tinged sputum. He then took a radical step of faith: he went out and stood on a little rock behind the hostel and called on Jesus the Christ, saying, *'Jesus, if it is true that you did all those miracles that I read about in the New Testament, do it again...*" From that day, he was free of tuberculosis and has lived in health thereafter.

On another occasion, while in his teens, he was moved by his mother's tears after his younger brother had suddenly slumped and died. He asked his mother to take his younger brother to a select part of the house, where he regularly prayed. Within five minutes, he gave his mother back her youngest son alive! That brother is today is a state Pastor of the Winners' Church, and, at the time of the miracle, signaled a sign of the future David Oyedepo had before him.

Today, Bishop Oyedepo is a "father" to thousands of pastors, and adviser to Presidents and Governors of nations. He is an accomplished businessman with a doctoral degree in human development, and has been blessed with thirty-four years of wedding bliss to his wife, Pastor Faith Oyedepo. They have four children, two of whom are actively serving in the ministry, and his testimony is one used by God to transform those who were formerly impoverished into the influential of society by the preaching of the word of faith.

Life Lesson 91: There is nothing impossible to those who believe!

God is the only one too big to fail!

Chapter Ninety-two

John Hagee's daughter: Healed of leiomyosarcoma of the lung

"Hear my cry, O God; attend unto my prayer. From the end of the earth will I cry unto thee, when my heart is overwhelmed: lead me to the rock that is higher than I" (Psalm 61:1-2).

John Hagee's oldest daughter, Tish, studied journalism and Spanish language, in her college years and afterwards became an integral part of the John Hagee ministry team for the past twenty years. She sings alongside her siblings in the John Hagee singers, helps with the translation of her father's books into Spanish, has published two books of her own including *Hear my cry* and *Master of the impossible* and continues to serve as wife and mother to the Tucker family she is married into..

In 2005, Tish had a persistent cough that would just not go away. She took over-the-counter medications and saw her family physician but the cough persisted. On further evaluation with an X-ray, a lung lesion was noted. After a Computerized Tomography (CT) scan of the chest localized the lesion, Tish underwent a bronchoscopy for pathological diagnosis.

The results were not what Tish or her family expected. The results showed Tish had a rare and very aggressive kind of malignant cancer, Leimyosarcoma of the lung. It has a high mortality rate, and doctors advised Tish and her family to prepare for the worst. They gave her about nine months to live, as it was considered a near-death sentence and had little hope in terms of prognosis.

Faith-fixed and fruitful

The drop of a needle could be heard in the room when the doctors told Tish her diagnosis, but John Hagee placed his hand on her and prayed over her the father's blessing. He proclaimed her blessed not cursed, and alive not dead. Tish had seen miracles of healing in her father's ministry, but now she needed to believe God for herself.

She decided to soak herself in His word daily and to recite only His promises to her. God then gave her a revelation from His word in Psalm 61:6. It says, God *"...wilt prolong the king's life: and his years as many generations."* Those words sparked off a holy hatred for premature death in Tish and spurred her divine desire for long life.

Ten years later, Tish is still alive and healthy. After undergoing experimental chemotherapy and radiation therapy, she is cancer-free and living her life to the full. She continues to work in the ministry, albeit more in the background, and goes around sharing her testimony and thanking God for His supernatural power that obliterated cancer from her body.

Life Lesson 92: A father's blessing is a *sine qua non* for long life!

It is not Over until God says it is over!

- Pastor Matthew Ashimolowo
(Snr. Pastor Kingsway International Christian
Center, London, United Kingdom)

Chapter Ninety-three

Eddie Jackson: Ministry and Medical Miracle Candidate!

"And whosoever shall give to drink unto one of these little ones a cup of cold water only in the name of a disciple, verily I say unto you, he shall in no wise lose his reward" (Matthew 10:42).

Eddie Jackson and his wife Betty have been strong advocates for the cause of children in the Monroe and West Monroe area. They have been pivotal to the upkeep of hundreds of children, and they continue till date to serve the children in the community as guardians and mentors.

As new converts to Christ, they started a seasonal Bible camp for children where they fed, clothed and serenaded children with love and attention they were lacking in majority of the homes represented.

Eddie is a military veteran with war experience in Vietnam. He started his own electrical company when he retired. As God prospered him, he supported several local and international causes, especially those concerning children. He also ministered on the radio and in prisons with the gospel of God's love for all.

Free at Last

In 2015, while preparing to go out to minister Eddie suddenly became unconscious. He was immediately rushed to a nearby community hospital where he was confirmed to have meningococcal disease with septicemia. The prognosis for his condition was poor, since less than 50% survive similar conditions without debilitating disease.

Medical personnel placed him on respiratory support for his compromised airway. He remained unconscious for another two weeks thereafter. They told Eddie's family that he had a near zero percent of full recovery and that even if he woke up from his comatose state, he would suffer severe neurological deficits.

Miraculously after a few weeks, Eddie regained consciousness and full control of his airway. To the shock of the attending medical staff, he remembered all surrounding circumstances and characters comprehensively and had full range of motion with intact cognition.

Today, Eddie is ambulating independently and has full independent rein physically, psychologically and spiritually. He still preaches on the radio and is assistant pastor of his local congregation. He is fully restored to health and cherishes his time with his family more than ever. Truly, he is free at last!

Life Lesson 93: First obtain His life; then watch the blessings flow!

"We don't know our future, but God does. And we know God!"

- Don Givler, MD, Associate professor Louisiana State University School of Medicine (Encouraging his wife, Amy, following her diagnosis with Hodgkin's lymphoma)

Chapter Ninety-four

Amy Givler's supernatural childbirth

"That they may teach the young women to be sober, to love their husbands, to love their children, to be discreet, chaste, keepers at home, good, obedient to their own husbands, that the word of God be not blasphemed" (Titus 2:4-5).

D on and Amy Givler are a blessing to the body of Christ. They have been married more than 35 years, have three lovely children, serve as physicians and part-time missionaries and have served as a rallying point for believers in the Arkansas, Louisiana and Mississippi area. Even though they met in Georgetown University, near Washington D.C, during medical school, their life story seems to emanate from Monroe, Louisiana more and more.

1n 1993, Amy's life was threatened by Hodgkin's lymphoma. She noticed some hard lumps on the right side of her neck. They were bigger than 2cm, sudden in onset but not associated with any weight loss, increased sweating or signs of infection. She asked for Don's opinion and when he said he was worried Amy really got concerned.

Within twenty-four hours, Amy Givler had a lymph node biopsy which demonstrated classic *reed-steinberg* cells positive for Hodgkin's lymphoma. This was all confounding to thirty-three year old Amy, but even more confounding was the fact that she was fifteen weeks pregnant with their third child!

Excising bad cells, early child birth and embracing His beauty

The turmoil, stress and emotional drainage from Hodgkin's lymphoma took a toll on Amy. She was initially scheduled to do six months of chemotherapy but it stretched to eight months instead. She was shut down physically, and psychologically she was tethering on the edge. Don and some family friends had to help her several times just to get her back on her feet to take the next round of chemotherapy.

Her faith was, however, strengthened throughout the ordeal. She read the Bible and any other inspirational books she could find. She also kept a journal for her thoughts. Through it all, she never grew bitter against the all-knowing and all-loving God but put her implicit trust in him.

The Givler's baby boy came in the seventh month, earlier than planned. Apart from a few weeks in the Neonatal Intensive Care Unit (NICU), baby David was well with no congenital deficits. This was noteworthy as Amy had undergone about twenty weeks of chemotherapy with little David in her womb.

Twenty-three years later, Amy is still cancer-free. She wrote a book titled *"Living with cancer"* that testifies of God's faithfulness throughout her one year of running back and forth for cancer treatment. She noticed that after her bout with cancer, she has now developed more compassion for those living with illnesses such as cancer.

Life Lesson 94: God said their weapons won't prosper, but that doesn't meant they won't be fashioned!

*You cannot possess what you
do not pursue, and it takes
yearning to acquire learning!*

Chapter Ninety-five

Marilyn Hickey: God's Signs and Wonders Woman!

*"...children are an heritage of the Lord: and the fruit
of the womb is his reward"* (Palm 127:3).

Marilyn Hickey at twenty-six years of age was sold out to Jesus Christ. She had given her life to Christ as a sixteen-year-old teen, been healed of an incurable disease at the age of eight, and married at twenty-three years of age an Assemblies of God preacher called Wally who inspired her to believe for more of God. Alongside her husband, Marilyn was committed to a life of ministry in the Colorado mountains.

While in Dallas, Texas, for a healing conference with William Branham in 1954, she had an encounter with the Supernatural that altered her destiny forever. She was called out of the audience by the man of God. He told her, *"You are not from here. You are from Denver, Colorado. You are from a wooded area, and you can't have a baby."*

He then told her, *"Go home and receive your child."* Meanwhile she knew because of an inherited condition she had, medical personnel had matter of factly told her she would never conceive and after three years of trying she and her husband had given up hope of having biological children. As Braham spoke to her, she said that she saw herself as if in a wheel within a wheel rising from below her feet into her feet and carrying her forth.

Marilyn went home to Denver, Colorado expectant; but after eight years of waiting for her miracle, she became despondent and adopted a child called Michael. Wally, her husband, however, refused to give up. He insisted William Braham's prophesy was for their own biological children and stood on God's word from Exodus 23:26.

From Orchard to Outreach

In 1960, Marilyn and Wally Hickey founded the Full Gospel Temple that later became Orchard Road Christian Center Denver, Colorado and at thirty-six years of age, Marilyn Hickey fulfilled the prophecy of William Braham and gave birth to her daughter, Sarah. The doctors were dumbfounded and speechless. To their medical mind, it was impossible for Marilyn to ever conceive and her delivery of this healthy child was to them nothing short of a miracle.

In 1980, God told Marilyn Hickey to *"cover the earth with the knowledge of God as the waters cover the seas"* (Isaiah 11:9) and Marilyn Hickey Ministries was born. From little beginnings, including small group Bible studies in her home, Marilyn has gone on to cover one hundred and thirty countries of the earth with the gospel. Sometimes, in hostile Moslem countries, she has preached to audiences of over four hundred thousand people at a time.

Today, at eighty-five years of age Marilyn has handed over leadership of the church to her son-in-law and daughter, Pastor and Mrs. Sarah Bowling. She still shares the spotlight on her daily television show with her now fifty-year-old-plus daughter, Sarah, as she broadcasts to a potential listening audience of 2.2 billion people daily.

Her testimony of supernatural healing has motivated her to take the gospel of signs and wonders all around the world. She believes the gospel of healing serves as evidence of the gospel to bring the heathen to the knowledge of Jesus. Her message, she says is one of love, not confrontation, and as a result she has been allowed to preach even in mosques with tens of thousands repenting.

Life Lesson 95: Faith does not just say God can; it also believes God will!

"Herein lies Lester Sumrall, a man who starved to death trusting God!"

- **Tombstone epitaph recommended by Lester Sumrall (1906-1987)** (In reply to San Francisco pastor who chided him for travelling the world on a global mission journey with only twelve dollars to his name).

Chapter Ninety-six

Lester Sumrall and the Strange Story of Clarita Villaneva

"The Spirit of the Lord is upon me, because he hath anointed me to preach the gospel to the poor; he hath sent me to heal the broken hearted, to preach deliverance to the captives, and recovering of sight to the blind, to set at liberty them that are bruised" (Luke 4:18).

C larita Villaneva was a Filipino orphan who when hawking her body on the streets of Manila, Philippines been arrested for prostitution. Her father had died at the age of two and her idolatrous and prostitution-promoting mother, who introduced Villaneva to the strange world of sorcery and sex, had also died suddenly just before her twelfth birthday.

From that day forward, Villaneva officially became a prostitute. She travelled extensively until she settled in the Philippines capital city of Manila. While there she continued to earnestly sell her body and to live a wayward life filled with drugs, alcohol and perverseness.

One night, at the age of eighteen, Clarita was attempting to curry a bystander for sex unaware the male prospect she was pursuing was a police officer. She was immediately arrested, incarcerated at the local city jail and charged with prostitution. Her freedom was momentarily lost, while incarcerated, but the events that were to follow would place her in perpetual freedom for the rest of her life!

In Jail and the Confused Jury!

Once Villaneva arrived at the prison, she began to scream and writhe in pain uncontrollably. She alleged that two spirit beings were biting her on her crotch and torso. Amazingly, onlookers including Father Benito Vargas of the Catholic Church, testified of seeing bite marks with saliva in them. These repeated incidents resulted in pure hysteria for Clarita.

The prison medical staff, led by Dr. Tara, were puzzled. They had no scientific explanations for these recurring incidents. As a result, they sent out feelers across the nation for scientific or religious answers, but nothing seemed to work! Some of the Christian leaders who were invited, feigned seemingly-impossible schedules to avoid confronting the now-severely tortured Clarita Villaneva.

The situation had generated much publicity in the media, especially after two highly placed officials of the prison died within twenty-four hours of incurring the wrath of Clarita. One day in May 1953, while working on a new building for his church, Lester Sumrall heard the strange story of Clarita Villaneva. The burden for this strange girl seized Lester, and he prayed for her all day and night in his home. It was then that God gave him a mandate concerning Villaneva that would live on in the memoirs of history world wide.

The Devil Is "Dead"

While praying for Clarita that night in May 1953, Lester Sumrall heard God tell him "If you will go to the jail and pray for her, I will deliver her." Lester, however, did not want to cast doubt on his heavily laundered reputation. He had just started a Church in the Manila area, and felt that going to the Bilibid Prison - where Clarita Villaneva was -, could jettison his hopes of a successful Church plant. He asked God to send someone else but God insisted on him and promised to use him mightily.

Enroute to the Bilibid Prison, Lester Sumrall decided to stop at the home of the Mayor and asked for permission to see and pray for Clarita

Villaneva. He had been introduced to the Mayor by a mutual friend, Architect Lepoldo Coronel, and the mayor in turn introduced Lester to the Prison's medical director – Dr. Lara.

After explaining his mission, which was witnessed by a myriad of newspaper journalists and onlookers, Lester went into a room to talk to Villaneva. She immediately challenged Lester and accused him of being a bastard. She then cursed and blasphemed the Godhead in English, even though Clarita Villaneva as an individual had no comprehension or ability to speak the English language.

This back and forth shouting match continued for upwards of forty-eight hours, and eventually Villaneva spoke in a soft gentle voice in her native tongue saying *"they have gone out of that window."* As Lester and his prayer partners were about to leave, however, the demons returned and spoke in perfect English language.

Again, Lester prayed and they departed albeit this time for good. The environment was awash with penitent sinners crying all around and Villaneva confessing Jesus as her Lord and Savior. The next day's newspaper headlines declared *"The Devil Is Dead"* and today Villaneva lives in the Northeastern part of the Philippines free from demonic oppression. The strange happenings propelled Lester Sumrall and his fledgling Church into the national spotlight. The Church, Cathedral of Praise, went to became one of the largest in the Asian region and spurred a revival in that part of the world.

Life Lesson 96: When God appears, the devil disappears!

Insanity is doing what you have always done, and expecting a different outcome!

-Albert Einstein (World renowned physicist)
(1879 - 1955)

Chapter Ninety-seven

David Remedios: From the Streets to the Stars!

"Pure religion and undefiled before God and the Father is this,
To visit the fatherless and widows in their affliction, and to
keep himself unspotted from the world" (James 1:27).

A t the age of Fifteen years, David Remedios lived on the streets of Manhattan, New York. He had run away from a broken and fractured home where he was abused and misused. For three years he lived on the streets of New York selling drugs and using alcohol. He was penniless and considered one of the vestiges of the Cuban-American society who have nothing to contribute.

On one fateful day, while walking down the dark and lonely streets of Manhattan at Fifteen years of age, he saw a tract on the side-walk. The tract talked about the finished work of Christ and after reading it, David surrendered his life to Christ. He had watched his life ebbing away on the streets of New York and after that decision for Christ made up his mind that change was necessary.

From that day forward, David was a new man. In between Church services and high school classes, David squatted with different families till he finished high school at Nineteen years of age. When he told his school guidance counselor he wanted to be a physician, they thought he was day-dreaming. They looked at his academic background, and told him pointblank he had no future in medicine but David persisted with his dream.

Soldier, Storm-raider and Spiritual general!

In 1977, David graduated from Hobart and Williams Smith college, New York city with a major in Pre-med and Biology. He had spent those four years studying like crazy, because he was determined to succeed and help his family. Even though he was often short of money and lacking in school supplies, he dug deep into his faith to overcome the obstacles straddling his path.

He was accepted into New York University (NYU) Medical School and offered a full-board scholarship if he would join the United States Air force (USAF) on graduation. He went on to specialize in general and vascular surgery at Baylor University Methodist hospital where he studied under great minds such as Dr. Debakey.

He served in the United States Air Force between 1988 and 1998 and got a bronze star for exemplary conduct in organizing multinational forces preparing for casualties in Riyadh, Saudi Arabia. After years of active service, Dr. Remedios retired to civilian practice in Monroe, Louisiana and active ministry as Pastor, teacher and apostolic leader at Trinity Christian Church in Forest Hill, Louisiana, USA.

Prior to his military career, David had married a young Puerto-Rican woman called Yvonne. Together they have five lovely children. In 2011, he pioneered the Louisiana Outpouring (LAO) Ministry that organizes outpouring conferences all around the country. He is frequently seen on several multiple media outlets and is currently a highly sought out speaker at international conferences, and television studios all around the world.

Life Lesson 97: Soon is God's signature, not later!

You will call one, and two hundred persons will answer!

- Mrs. Adeboye (mother to Pastor E.A. Adeboye)
(declaring covenant blessings over her-then teenage son)

Chapter Ninety-eight

E.A Adeboye: Terrible to the Enemy, Terrific to the Elect!

"Enoch walked with God: and he was not; for God took him" (Genesis 5:24).

Pastor E.A Adeboye is pastor of the largest congregation on the planet at the Redeemed Christian Church of God (RCCG). Gatherings of more than seven million people at the Holy Ghost Convocation of RCCG have been recorded. Their monthly Holy Ghost Night prayer vigils on the Lagos-Ibadan expressway are some of the largest gatherings in the world.

After a stellar academic career at University of Nigeria, Ife, Lagos and Ilorin Pastor Adeboye obtained a doctorate in hydro-dynamic mathematics in 1975. He had endured poverty as a child; and with a relatively improved wealth status, he began to distance himself from the God he served as a youth.

He, however, became a Christian in 1973 under the leadership of Pastor Josiah Akindayomi – the founder of RCCG – while he was seeking healing for a mysterious disease troubling his wife, Foluke. She had been told she could have no more children as a result of her pelvic bones structure.

After the prayers of Pastor Akindayomi, Sister Foluke gave birth to two more children, bringing the total number of children born to the Adeboye family to four. Foluke Adeboye's healing triggered faith in Pastor E.A. Adeboye's heart, and he began to see miracles, healings and deliverance in his ministry.

Father to Plenty, Friend of Presidents and Fervent Preacher of the word

The journey of Pastor Adeboye at the RCCG has been a virtuoso experience. He started as English interpreter for the Yoruba-speaking Akindayomi in 1973. He was then ordained a pastor in 1975, became the General Overseer in 1981 at the death of Pastor Akindayomi in 1980 and within thirty years transformed RCCG into the fastest growing Church in the world with over thirty thousand branches in over two hundred countries.

He also founded the Christ the Redeemer's Ministries, as a body of protégés who will support the cause of Christ around the world. This body today consists of some of Nigeria's leading ministers' including Bishop Oyedepo, Pastor Kure and Wale Oke who consider Pastor Adeboye a mentor and spiritual father.

He attracted young and affluent members to the RCCG, by broadening the music and style of worship. He introduced model parishes into the RCCG structure and within a few years saw the *crème-de-la crème* of society falling over themselves to belong to the RCCG. Politicians, traditional rulers and movie stars covet his relationship, and along side members of his Church are a current vice-president of Nigeria, state governors and a plethora of senators and legislators.

His interest in soul winning is non-abating. His ministry organizes a "Let us go fishing" outreach monthly that seeks the wicked, woe be gone and worthless members of society such as street urchins, prostitutes and drug dealers. He introduced international standards to media ministry in Nigeria with the introduction of live streaming through the RCCG owned TV/Radio Dove media stations.

He is considered one of the most influential Africans on earth, and is a regular visitor to international agencies like the United Nations. His emphasis, however, has remained holiness and simply obeying the instructions of God without theatrics or maneuvering. He commands a following like no other in the world and has private jets and a financial arsenal to go with it. Notwithstanding all that, however, he remains the epitome of humility and holiness.

Life Lesson 98: God does not bless our works; He blesses His works commissioned for our hands to carry out!

"Raise up your students to hear My voice, to go where My light is dim, where My voice is heard small, and My healing power is not known, even to the uttermost bounds of the earth. Their work will exceed yours, and in this I am well pleased"

- God's commission to Oral Roberts (1918 – 2009) in 1963 at the launch of Oral Roberts University (ORU).

Chapter Ninety-nine

Oral Roberts: Healed from Tuberculosis

"Blessed be God, even the Father of our Lord Jesus Christ, the Father of mercies, and the God of all comfort; Who comforteth us in all our tribulation, that we may be able to comfort them which are in any trouble, by the comfort wherewith we ourselves are comforted of God" (2 Corinthians 1:3-4).

Oral Roberts, at the age of seventeen, was dying from tuberculosis in Enid, Oklahoma. He had been coughing up blood, was feverish and increasingly weak for more than a year. In 1935, when Oral was suffering from Tuberculosis, his condition was considered a death sentence. He and his family, of which he was the fifth of six children, were simply told to take him home to die as his condition was incurable.

As he lay dying in his bed that night in 1935, the Lord God spoke to young Oral. He told him, *"Son, I am going to heal you, and you are to take my healing power to your generation. And someday, you are to build me a university based on my authority and on the Holy Spirit."*

That very night Oral's brother drove him to a tent revival in Ada, Oklahoma. At the crusade, evangelist George Moncey laid his hands on Oral's body and prayed that the foul tormenting disease in Oral's body come out of him and let him be free from disease in the name of Jesus.

The power of God fell on Oral, and he was healed instantly. Not only were his lungs healed from that day on, but the stutter that had characterized Oral's speaking was also gone! His life was forever changed, and the birth of Oral Roberts Ministry had begun.

Commissioned to Change His World

Oral Roberts started his preaching ministry after that healing visitation. He served as pastor of two churches in the Georgia and Oklahoma International Pentecostal Holiness Districts between 1941 and 1947. In May 1947, he conducted his first crusade at Enid, Oklahoma, with over twelve hundred people in attendance. Testimonies out of that meeting heralded the launch in Tulsa, Oklahoma, of the Oral Roberts Ministries in 1948, the Abundant Life Prayer Group in 1959, the Oral Roberts University in 1962, and the Golden Eagle Broadcasting Studios in 1983.

He travelled to over fifty-six countries with the healing power of Jesus, conducted over three hundred open-air crusades, and personally laid hands on more than two million people with testimonies of miraculous healings following. His passion for healing was infectious and it was said to be inspired by his early life experience with tuberculosis. He coined the phrase "Go into every man's world" and as a pioneer of the healing movement popularized the integration of healing and medicine with the establishment of the City of Faith Medical Complex in 1981.

His life story would be incomplete without talking about his dutiful partner, Evelyn Roberts (1938 – 2005), who supported him throughout his ministry and with whom he had four children. Two of their children, Rebecca Nash and Ronald Roberts, died prematurely but through it all Oral remained resolute in believing God for miracles and standing strong on God's word. He built the first truly charismatic inter-denominational ministry that traversed race, denomination, social class or creed. His legacy lives on in the $600 million, 35-acre ORU Campus that continues to produce Christian world leaders that are filled with the spirit of God and the urgency for souls in diverse fields of human endeavor.

Life Lesson 99: God is coming for a glorious, not a garbage, church!

Many who want to be healed externally must first be healed internally to be truly made whole!

Chapter One Hundred

Dr. Jesse Duplantis and God's Surgery

"I beseech you therefore, brethren, by the mercies of God, that ye present your bodies a living sacrifice, holy, acceptable unto God, which is your reasonable service. And be not conformed to this world: but be ye transformed by the renewing of your mind, that ye may prove what is that good, and acceptable, and perfect, will of God" (Romans 12:1-2).

D r. Jesse Duplantis is one of America's most beloved pastors. He currently shepherds the Jesse Duplantis Ministries and Covenant Church Destrehan, Louisiana, in the United State of America. His messages are full of joy, hilarious laughter, and deep spiritual insight.

At the Believers' Faith Convention in 2014, Jesse Duplantis spoke about how God recently asked him to go to a top heart doctor in the New Orleans area of Louisiana because he had a heart condition that needed therapy. He saw the cardiac specialist who conducted echocardiograms and stress tests on his heart. Medical personnel told him his heart was fine and that he had nothing to worry about.

He, however, insisted and asked them about the possibility of missing other heart conditions through these already performed investigations and they answered in the affirmative. They said the definitive diagnostic tool was a cardiac catheterization test and Jesse immediately offered to do it the next day.

Living life to the full till it overflows

After undergoing cardiac catheterization, the cardiologists identified a defective heart valve that needed urgent surgical attention. They performed open heart surgery, repaired the defective heart valve and within three days Jesse Duplantis was discharged from the hospital.

The consequence of not repairing that heart valve could have been grave. Ultimately, through the promptings of the Holy Spirit, God ensured Jesse's heart remains strong for future ministry.

Today, Jesse is back to a full-schedule ministry and his confidence in God is as high as ever. He went through what others considered dangerous and life-threatening, without being flapped and regained his strength super quick because he stayed in tune with God.

Life lesson 100: If God promises, He will perform.

Contacts

This ministry, Faith and Power Ministries, is dedicated to showing the power of God once again to this generation. It is dedicated to ushering in the last days' glory of God and, in the course of doing so, turning lives around for the kingdom of God.

Our email is tobemomah@yahoo.com. We can be contacted via email or via our websites www.tobemomah.com or on www.faithandpowerministries.org. I currently reside in West Monroe, Louisiana and can be reached at P.O Box 550 West Monroe, Louisiana 71294 U.S.A.

Other Books by the Author

1. **Tobe Momah.** *A General and a gentleman* (biography of General Sam Momah) –Spectrum books 2003
2. **Tobe Momah.** *Between the systems, soul and spirit of man* (a Christian doctors view on sickness and its source) – Xulon press 2007
3. **Tobe Momah.** *Building lasting relationships* (a Manual for the complete home) – Xulon press 2006
4. **Tobe Momah.** *Metrobiology – A Study of life in the city* 1ST ed (a Doctor's Daily Devotional) – Xulon Press 2008
5. **Tobe Momah.** *Pregnancy: Pitfalls, Pearls and principles* – Westbow Press 2011
6. **Tobe Momah.** *Ultimate Harvest: Five F.A.C.T.S on Fruitfulness and how to grow the American Church again* - Westbow Press 2012
7. **Tobe Momah.** *From Edginess to Eagerness...taking the Church back to willing service* - Westbow Press 2012
8. **Tobe Momah.** *Fear no Evil...by hating evil* - Westbow Press 2013
9. **Tobe Momah.** *Fear no Evil...by hating evil (A daily devotional)* - Westbow Press - 2013
10. **Tobe Momah.** *S.T.E.P,S to the altar ...Why a glorious generation is living ashamed at the altar* - Westbow Press - 2014
11. **Tobe Momah.** *Healing Lives...True Stories of Encouragement and achievement in the midst of sickness!* Westbow Press – 2014.
12. **Tobe Momah.** *Stay In Tune (S.I.T)...Challenging an always going but Godless culture!* – Advanced Global Publishing 2015
13. **Tobe Momah.** *Stay In Tune (S.I.T)...Living Daily in His Presence (a Daily Devotional)* – Advanced Global Publishing 2015.

14. **Tobe Momah**. *The Death Knell called Depression!* – Advanced Global Publishing 2015.
15. **Tobe Momah**. *Heirs not Helpers: Raising a generation of plunderers who are not just pleaders*. Advanced Global Publishing 2015.
16. **Tobe Momah**. *Loyalty Legends... living a life of abundance through the anointing!* Westbow 2016.

Printed in the United States
By Bookmasters